■ ■ ■ ■ ■ ■ ■ ■ ■ ■ **A COMPLETE GUIDE** ■ ■ ■ ■ ■ ■ ■ ■ ■

Mount St. Helens
National Volcanic Monument

For HIKING,
SKIING, CLIMBING
& NATURE VIEWING

Klindt Vielbig

THE
MOUNTAINEERS

Published by
The Mountaineers
1001 SW Klickitat Way, Suite 201
Seattle, WA 98134

© 1997 by Klindt Vielbig

First edition 1987. Second edition: first printing 1996, second printing 1998

Published simultaneously in Great Britain by Cordee, 3a DeMontfort Street, Leicester, England, LE1 7HD   .

Manufactured in the United States of America

Edited by Heath Silberfeld
Maps by Jerry Painter
All photographs by the author, unless otherwise noted
Cover design by Patrick Lanfear and Helen Cherullo
Book design and typography by Alice C. Merrill
Book layout by Sandy Wing

Cover photographs: Main image: *Beargrass and Mount St. Helens* © Bob and Ira Spring. Insets, left to right: *Backpacker taking in scenery* © Milan Chuckovich, Tony Stone Images; *Mount St. Helens Visitor Center at Clearwater Ridge* © Nick Gunderson, Tony Stone Images; *Recovering vegetation and fallen trees* © John Marshall, Tony Stone Images
Frontispiece: *Muddy River Lahar on the east side of Mount St. Helens*

Library of Congress Cataloging-in-Publication Data
Vielbig, Klindt.
    A complete guide to Mount St. Helens National Volcanic Monument : for hikers, skiers, climbers, nature viewers / Klindt Vielbig.
        p.   cm.
    Includes index.
    ISBN 0-89886-503-4
    1. Outdoor recreation—Washington (State)—Mount Saint Helens National Volcanic Monument—Guidebooks. 2. Hiking—Washington (State)—Mount Saint Helens National Volcanic Monument—Guidebooks. 3 Skis and skiing—Washington (State)—Mount Saint Helens National Volcanic Monument—Guidebooks. 4. Nature study—Washington (State)—Mount Saint Helens National Volcanic Monument—Guidebooks. 5. Trails—Washington (State)—Mount Saint Helens National Volcanic Monument—Guidebooks. 6. Mount Saint Helens National Volcanic Monument (Wash.)—Guidebooks. I. Title.
GV191.42.W2V54   1997
917.97'84—dc21
                                                      96-52473
                                                      CIP

■ ■ ■ ■ ■ ■ ■

This book is dedicated to those who fought for years against great odds to establish monument status for the Mount St. Helens area, then battled against having the area they proposed reduced in size by economic and bureaucratic interests. The principle persons were Susan Saul, Noel McRae, Charlie Raines, and Russ Jolley. In addition, appreciation is shown to U.S. Congressmen Don Bonker and Sid Morrison, members of the Willapa Hills Audubon Society, and Brock Evans for their valuable efforts.

Contents

■ ■

MOUNT ST. HELENS NORTH   141

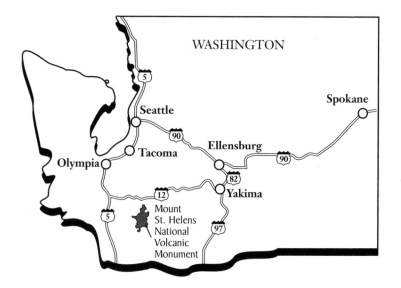

Introduction

■■■■■■■■■■■■■■■■■■■■■■■■■■■■■■■

Those of us who knew Mount St. Helens before the catastrophic eruption of May 1980 completely altered the landscape remember a beautiful lake surrounded by deep forests with the perfect snow cone of the mountain rising to the southwest. We have childhood memories of youth camps along the lakeshore and of the rustic buildings at Harmony Falls. Many of us climbed the mountain by the Dogshead route and hiked the long trail through forest up onto the high meadows of Mount Margaret, where resident—and territorial—mountain goats were often seen.

As we return to the mountain these memories linger, but now we must rediscover this landscape with few landmarks from bygone days. The volcanic explosion destroyed 150 square miles of forest and damaged 230 square miles of surrounding land. The area as far as 5 miles north of the volcano was devastated, buried by 500 feet of rock and debris. The scene now is like no other in the country, or indeed the world. There are stretches of barren land strewn with avalanche debris, ash, and pumice; scoured hillsides swept clear of trees; and craters formed by violent blasts of glacier ice.

More surprising than the lingering signs of volcanic destruction is the regeneration seen in this landscape. Immediately after the eruption, when vast areas were covered with ash, it was believed that the desolate, gray landscape would take many decades to renew itself and show signs of life. The recovery has been surprisingly fast; within three years of the blast, 90 percent of the plants and animals had returned. Today, vast hillsides of green populated with many plant species delight the visitor, and elk, bear, coyote, and numerous types of bird are present.

The monument has used no artificial means to reintroduce plants or species. The change and renewal have been achieved with no human interference whatsoever. Mount St. Helens National Volcanic Monument showcases the natural regeneration of an ecosystem after its near annihilation, and scientists from around the world come to observe the transformation of the landscape seen in this natural laboratory.

This landscape will continue to alter in years to come. Mount St. Helens is a young, active volcano, and future eruptions are inevitable. But until she blows again, the land around this mountain will continue to bring forth more and more life. The monument is a testament to the awesome power of nature, a place of paradox where destruction has given birth to magnificent formations, scarred plains, and delicate new meadows. This guide will help you understand the forces that continue to shape this dynamic place and show you where to go to best appreciate its ever-changing beauty.

▪ HISTORY ▪

Ancient Stories

Native Americans inhabited the area surrounding Mount St. Helens for some 12,000 years prior to the arrival of Europeans. Much of the land in close proximity to the mountain was rugged, and there is no record of settlement on the slopes of the volcano itself. The mid-Columbian Cowlitz and Klickitat peoples visited the foothills of St. Helens seasonally to hunt, fish, and pick berries, rarely venturing above timberline. Their names for Mount St. Helens reflect its explosive past—*Loowit*, Lady of Fire; *Tah-one-lat-clah*, Fire Mountain; and *La-we-lat-klat*, Person from Whom Smoke Comes.

A number of native legends, all featuring the same cast of characters, surround the three major volcanoes of northern Oregon and southern Washington—Mount Hood, Mount Adams, and Mount St. Helens. Hood

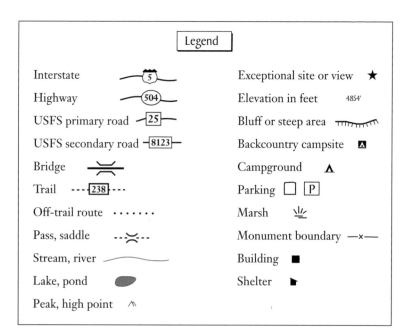

Legend	
Interstate	Exceptional site or view ★
Highway	Elevation in feet 4854'
USFS primary road	Bluff or steep area
USFS secondary road	Backcountry campsite ◣
Bridge	Campground ▲
Trail	Parking ☐ P
Off-trail route	Marsh
Pass, saddle	Monument boundary —x—
Stream, river	Building ■
Lake, pond	Shelter ▶
Peak, high point	

and Adams are the male warrior peaks, fighting each other for the beautiful *Loowit*. Their battles involve fire, smoke, and throwing rocks. The ancient stories of the mountain portray it as a powerful, dangerous, and spiritual place. It was not for human habitation, and one would do well to keep a respectful distance from it.

One legend tells us that Spirit Lake, at the foot of beautiful *Loowit*, is home to the *seeahtiks*. Neither human nor animal, *seeahtiks*

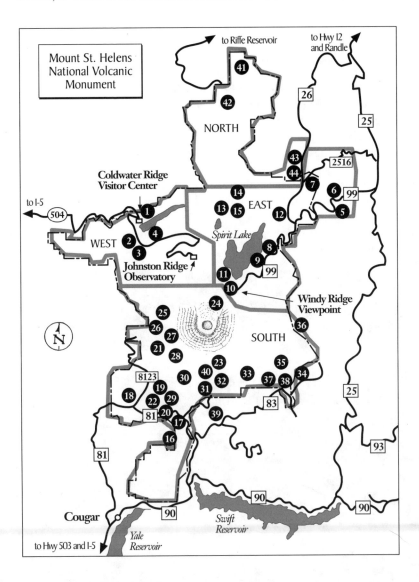

are big-breasted, giant, shaggy monsters. This tale was probably suffi-ciently fearsome to discourage most Indians from exploring the Spirit Lake basin. The story goes on to describe how unfortunate explorers of the area, following an elk or deer into the dangerous, spirit-inhab-ited region, were caught by the *seeahtiks*, who reached their long arms from the lake to pull the unwary hunters below the surface. Only the strongest could survive. A few braves would, however, deliberately ven-ture into the treacherous region to seek their *tamanaweis*, their soul power, and would return endowed with spirit strength.

European Settlement and Development

The first European sighting of the mountain was recorded in 1792 by Captain George Vancouver, who named it for Alleyne Fitzherbert, Brit-ish ambassador to the Court of Madrid and lord of a small city near Liverpool called Saint Helens. The next group to make mention of the mountain was the Lewis and Clark Expedition in 1805.

The earliest known ascent of St. Helens was made in August 1853 by a group led by Thomas J. Dryer. The trip by horseback took two weeks and went up the Lewis River Valley to the south slopes of the mountain, where the party witnessed smoke escaping from the peak.

Elk tracks near Pleasant Pass, a common sight in the monument north of Mount St. Helens in the blast zone

The town of Toutle 40 miles west of the mountain was established in 1876. Logging began, and miners explored the area in the 1890s. In 1901 a wagon road was built to Spirit Lake to support commerce in the area. Although a great deal of effort was expended in prospecting for minerals, the mines were not successful and closed in a few years.

The scenic beauty of the area soon attracted visitors for recreational purposes, and beginning in 1913 four youth camps were built along the shores of the lake. Public campgrounds and resorts followed, and soon many private cabins were built. In 1946, the road to the lake was paved and more visitors came.

The Battle for the Land

In 1890 Mount St. Helens was included in a forest preserve, and in 1908 it became part of the Columbia National Forest (later the Gifford Pinchot National Forest). The management of the region's lands by the U.S. Forest Service resulted in extensive clearcutting. As early as 1969, conservationists, alarmed by the destruction, pushed to have the mountain protected within a scenic preserve or monument under the control of the National Park Service. The Forest Service maintained that timber harvesting was an economic necessity. By 1975, 2,300 miles of roads crisscrossed the national forest's lands and few roadless areas remained.

To complicate the management of resources, the checkerboard pattern of private ownership of land meant that square-mile sections alternated with federal lands. In the late 1800s the government had given land grants to railroads to encourage railroad construction. Burlington Northern Railroad was the prime beneficiary, even owning the very summit of St. Helens. Other large private landholdings were owned by Weyerhaeuser and Champion International, both still dominant players today in the timber industry on the periphery of the monument. Dams were built on the nearby Lewis River for power generation. Resources around the mountain were being damaged at an alarming rate.

Conservationists battling the powerful opposition of the Forest Service and private landholders included the Mount St. Helens Protective Association. Overuse of the Green River Valley was one of their first causes. Noel McRae and Russ Jolley plotted a strategy to protect unique areas of old-growth forest. They received little response to concerns for proposed logging in the Ghost Lake area on the western slope of Strawberry Mountain 12 miles northeast of St. Helens. They fought to reduce damaging road construction—with its effects on streams and salmon—and the introduction of heavy recreation in fragile areas. But it soon became apparent that fighting a timber sale or two was insufficient, so McRae's goal became to create a Mount St. Helens National Monument. The Ghost Lake timber sale was finally stopped in 1973, eliminating the building of roads on fragile soils.

It took five years to save the Green River Valley and preserve access to the Mount Margaret backcountry 8 miles north of St. Helens, but more logging issues re-emerged, so McRae and Susan Saul, as co-chairpersons, revitalized the Mount St. Helens Protective Association. St. Helens was passed over in 1979 for wilderness status, a great disappointment after so much effort. In fact, the Strawberry Mountain area was designated "multiple use" and logging stripped its western slopes above the Green River Valley.

After the 1980 eruption Saul and McRae proposed an enlarged area for monument status, supported by many groups. Timber interests opposed the size, reducing it to only the blast zone. Finally, 18 months later President Reagan signed an enlarged monument bill creating a 110,000-acre preserve.

The Eruptions

The 40,000-year geological history of Mount St. Helens includes explosive eruptions, pyroclastic flows, lava flows, and lava domes that have been blasted away and rebuilt several times. She has erupted fourteen times in the last 4,000 years, twice as often as Mount Shasta, the second most active of the Cascade volcanoes. There have been periods of hundreds of years during which the mountain was active, as well as long periods of dormancy. Five hundred years ago St. Helens erupted violently and lava flows were ejected with ash blowing as far as Canada. Dome building followed this, resulting in the beautiful, symmetrical shape of pre-1980. About 200 years ago an explosive eruption occurred, followed by a quiet period with only four small eruptions in the early to mid-1800s.

The volcano reawakened with earthquakes on March 20, 1980, after 123 years of dormancy. On March 27, it produced a steam eruption. The upper northside slopes and summit area slowly became distorted by pressure from magma (liquid or molten rock) within the mountain. A huge bulge was created and grew steadily, while large steaming craters formed in the summit snow and ice fields. The bulge continued to grow, and it became evident that this out-of-balance mass could break loose. This is precisely what happened when the frequent earthquakes caused by moving magma deep below the mountain finally precipitated the collapse of the mountain's north side.

St. Helens erupted cataclysmically on May 18, 1980, at 8:32 A.M.

Aerial looking south at Mount St. Helens and Mount Hood with Harry's Ridge and Johnston Ridge in the foreground. St. Helens and Spirit Lakes are seen to the left. The Pumice Plain is at the foot of mountain and the Plains of Abraham are on the mountain's shoulder. (Austin Post, U.S. Geological Survey)

The eruption resulted in a huge landslide, an explosive lateral blast, numerous pyroclastic flows, devastating volcanic debris flows, and mudflows called lahars that flowed down river valleys. A tremendous tephra plume of ash and rocks of all sizes was ejected into the stratosphere for more than nine hours and rose 12 miles. The ash column formed a mushroom cloud 45 miles across, and ash circled the earth.

The debris avalanche was the largest landslide in recorded history and left hummocks (enormous mounds of avalanche debris from the landslide and rock from the summit and crater of the mountain) and other deposits up to 500 feet deep over miles of terrain at the north foot of the mountain. The landslide avalanche hit Spirit Lake, creating a gigantic wave that swept the length of the lake, rising on the lake's mountainside walls as high as 800 feet above the original level of the lake. The wave swept all soil, all vegetation, and enormous numbers of old-growth trees from the lake's sides. The avalanche debris raised the lake's surface to its present level 180 feet above the original level, and greatly expanded the lake's size.

Mudflows were carried down both the North and South Forks of the Toutle River, causing great damage to miles of highways and roads, taking out bridges, destroying over 300 homes, and carrying sediment 70 miles to the Columbia River, where river traffic was affected for almost three months until dredging cleared the channel. Mudflows swept down all sides of the mountain, mixing with and melting snowfields and lowering glacier surfaces by 24 feet. The Muddy River flats up to a mile wide had a mudflow over 30 feet deep that traveled down Pine Creek and the Muddy River to the Lewis River and deposited huge numbers of trees into Swift Reservoir. Thousands of elk, deer, and mountain goats were killed. Fifty-seven people died, most from heat and ash asphyxiation. The death count would have been much higher had the eruption not occurred on a Sunday, as loggers were working weekdays in the vicinity on Weyerhaeuser lands. The amount of rock and volcanic debris lost and ejected in the explosion would fill an area the size of a football field to a height of 62 miles. The amount of eruption material was twice the amount that buried Pompeii.

Five additional explosive eruptions followed during the summer and fall of 1980, producing ash plumes that reached altitudes of 4 to 8 miles and numerous pyroclastic flows. The enormous crater, 2,000 feet deep and over a mile wide, gave rise to a lava dome during 17 eruptive periods until 1986. The dome grew to a height of almost 1,000 feet in height and 2,000 feet in width. There has been no dome growth for several years.

In February 1996 heavy rainfalls and rapid melting of deep snowpacks produced record flooding west of the Cascades. Millions of tons of ash and logs were swept into the monument's waterways. The dramatic flooding caused great damage to streams and riparian areas, and many landslides resulted from saturated hillsides, causing extensive damage to trails and roads. As disastrous as this was, it was just another event in a long cycle of natural disturbances from which plant and animal communities eventually recover.

■■■■■■■■■■■■■■■■■■■■■■■■■■■■■■■■■■■■■■■

Geology and the Cascade Mountains

The Cascade Range stretches some 700 miles north to south, from Garibaldi in southern British Columbia to Lassen in northern California. These grand mountains, of an average height of 4,000 to 5,000 feet, include twenty-two prominent volcanic peaks. The range is geologically young: while the nearby Olympics and the Coast Range of Oregon are approximately 45 million years old, the Cascades are only about 6 million years old. To understand how this range was formed, a brief description of geological processes may be helpful.

The crust of the earth, the layer we live on, is relatively solid and varies in thickness, averaging about 25 miles. Under the crust is the mantle, a layer of hot, dense material that separates the crust from the earth's molten core. Convection currents arising within the mantle cause the crust to move and break apart into individual segments called tectonic plates. When these plates collide, the resulting pressure slowly (over millions of years) pushes the crust upward, forming mountain ranges. When two plates meet and the leading edge of one is forced under the edge of the other, a so-called subduction zone is created. In a subduction zone, the sinking plate is forced down into the mantle, where it melts and creates pools of magma that give rise to volcanoes and other volcanic phenomena.

The Cascades were created in just this fashion as the floor of the Pacific ocean (oceanic plate) moved eastward and slid under the continental plate of North America. The volcanic peaks and thousands of cinder cones found in the Cascade Range are the result of trapped magma in this subduction zone making its way to the surface.

There are several types of volcanoes. Mount Rainier, Mount Adams, Mount St. Helens, and the other prominent Cascade volcanoes are stratovolcanoes, whose cone-shaped peaks are made up of layers of lava, ash, or mud. Stratovolcanoes usually eject viscous, slow-moving lava (such as is seen on the south and east sides of St. Helens). Their eruptions can be violent, as were those of Mount Lassen in 1915, Mount Mazama many thousands of years ago (when a caldera was formed that eventually became Crater Lake), and St. Helens in 1980. Stratovolcanoes often erupt steam mixed with ash. The steam is created when water from melting snow and ice comes into contact with the hot magma, while the ash results from the decomposition of rocks inside the neck of the volcano. Another feature of stratovolcano eruptions is the occurrence of mudflows, or "lahars" (an Indonesian term for a mixture of rock, ash, debris, and water that may flow for miles with great destructive force), a phenomenon that is also clearly visible at St. Helens.

Shield volcanoes are formed when liquid lava flows quickly from a source vent and solidifies in low-lying concentric rings; the result looks like a shield, hence the name. Cinder cones are hills created when cinders and other pyroclastic (explosive) materials pile up around a volcanic vent. Both shield volcanoes and cinder cones are found throughout the Cascades; many of these are extinct and forested and thus more difficult to identify than their more famous cousins.

During a period that began about 1 million years ago and lasted until the end of the Pleistocene epoch about 10,000 years ago, alpine glaciers advanced and retreated throughout the mountain ranges of the Northwest. These sheets of ice carved and shaped the volcanoes of the Cascades; the evidence left by successive waves of glaciation often provides clues to a volcano's age. St. Helens is the youngest of Washington's volcanoes and the nearly perfect symmetry of its pre-1980 cone showed that it underwent less glacial shaping than older peaks such as Mount Rainier.

The Cascades are just a small part of the Pacific "Ring of Fire," a chain of about 1,300 volcanoes stretching from South America, through Central and North America, across the Aleutian Islands of Alaska, through eastern Russia, Japan, Indonesia, some South Pacific islands, New Zealand, and Antartica.

▪ THE MONUMENT TODAY ▪

Mount St. Helens National Volcanic Monument attracts more than 3 million visitors annually. To meet the public demand, roads leading into the heart of the monument from the east and west have been constructed. Hiking trails and three Forest Service visitor centers have been built to provide educational displays and information on the area's history, eruption, and ecosystem recovery.

Scarred tree damaged in 1980 lahar mudflow floods down Lava Canyon, thirty feet above present stream level

The monument is not large. It has an irregular shape and stretches 26 miles from north to south, 16 miles east to west at its widest, and 0.5 mile east to west at its narrowest. Its elevations vary from 600 feet near the town of Cougar to 8,365 feet at the summit of St. Helens. Surprisingly, although St. Helens is a massive, major volcano, its summit ranks as only the fiftieth-highest point in Washington State and the lowest of the five volcanoes in Washington State.

The many opportunities for activities around the monument are detailed below in How to Use This Book. The trail descriptions in this book were written after the 1996 floods, when numerous roads were closed due to flood damage. Most of these roads will be repaired and reopened by 1997. Since weather will continue to affect the monument, travelers should always obtain current information on road and trail conditions and closures.

Note that there are no campgrounds within the monument. Private, state, and national forest campgrounds can be found near the monument boundary. Refer to the appendix for information on state campground reservations. The visitor centers have information on all campgrounds in the vicinity. The north and south sides have several excellent campgrounds. Dispersed camping in undeveloped sites is permitted within the monument. No open fires are allowed in the blow-down forest, only camp stoves. On the south side of the mountain, many undeveloped, dispersed campsites are located on FR 81, FR 8123, FR 83, and at the Climber's Bivouac on FR 830. There is no water at these sites. On the west side, the most visited side, a state park is located across the highway from the Mount St. Helens Visitor Center 5 miles east of I-5.

Plants and Animals

During the first years after 1980, recovery was dominated by surviving plants resprouting through the ash and pumice and by buried plants being exposed by erosion. Surviving plants were soon joined by colonizing species that arrived from wind-blown seeds, many taking root in leaf mulch and shade provided by established plants. Birds and other animals have introduced other species. Many shrubs and trees have arisen, such as red alder, black cottonwood, and willow, particularly along stream courses and pond margins.

Scientists have established research plots in many areas to study the return and growth of plant life. A number of these are found in the Winds of Change Trail area west of the Coldwater Ridge Visitor Center. Others are in areas heavily used by elk. Large plots are fenced off and results compared year by year with an adjacent, unfenced "control" plot. Other study areas are on the Pumice Plain, the desert below and north of the crater, where temperatures of up to 1,100 degrees Fahrenheit killed all life and a few plants now struggle to return. Forest edge areas are also being studied for the long-term return of trees.

What you will see will depend on the ecological niche you are visiting. In the lowland conifer forests you will see fewer varieties of flowers and less color. However, in early summer there are trillium, Queen's cup, and avalanche lilies. The ground is often covered with vanilla leaf, ginger, oxalis, and a variety of ferns. Watch for bunchberries—a ground-hugging member of the dogwood family. The familiar, if smaller, dogwood flowers are followed in the fall by a cluster of bright red berries. In late summer, many areas contain several varieties of huckleberries.

In higher, dry, mid-zone areas one finds deep-rooted plants with leathery leaves or hairy leaves that retain moisture. Others here are penstemon, Indian paintbrush, gentian, lupine, mats of kinnikinnick, and manzanita. At or above timberline you will find in addition bear grass, cat's ears, pasque flower, heather, and phlox. You may find flat, ash-covered shores of the backcountry lakes beginning to be covered by partridge foot, dwarf raspberries, and wild strawberries.

In the lower elevations, the principal trees are maple, Douglas fir, cedar, and noble fir. Pacific silver fir, lodgepole pine, and subalpine fir are also found, as are willow and alder alongside streams.

The largest common animal in the monument is the elk, present in herds in all parts. Elk tracks appear on every trail, hillside, and saddle, but the animals themselves may not be seen unless hikers are quiet and scan the hillsides and valleys carefully. Deer are abundant but seldom seen. Before the eruption, mountain goats lived in the Mount Margaret area. Only one has been sighted since the eruption. Coyotes and bears are also present but seldom seen. During the berry season purple scat piles on trails indicate bear presence, and coyote scats composed of hair and bits of bone are commonly seen on trails. The presence of pocket gophers is made known by the dirt tubes wriggling across meadows, left behind from winter tunneling under the snow.

Numerous birds populate the monument. The varied thrush produces a long, eerie wavering note, followed by a lower or higher note. In the higher country, curious hummingbirds often approach closely with bulletlike speed. Ravens, often in pairs, are regularly seen performing joyful aerial acrobatics. The presence of owls is revealed by their pellets, sometimes regurgitated on trails, which are similar in content to coyote scat.

As prolific as many species appear to be, the monument visitor, multiplied by many thousand, can create thoughtless damage to nature just by picking a flower or crushing a plant underfoot. What has taken a decade to establish can be carelessly erased in a moment. Picking flowers, collecting rocks, or trampling plants by walking off-trail will alter the process of natural recovery, and all are against monument regulations. Please stay on trails and roads and be especially careful in the fragile areas of ash, sand, and pumice.

Visitor Centers

Offering dramatic views of St. Helens and the volcanic landscapes, the visitor centers are popular attractions. All are located on State Highway 504, the Spirit Lake Memorial Highway, which ends at the Johnston Ridge Observatory. They provide important information, including maps, and many have excellent educational displays and short interpretive walks through representative monument landscapes.

Mount St. Helens Visitor Center (at Silver Lake). This main visitor center sits only 5 miles east of I-5 and contains excellent exhibits on the cultural history, geology, and volcanology of the region, as well as the 1980 eruption, its effects on the landscape and ecosystems, and the return and regeneration of life. Audiovisual programs are presented frequently, and the gift shop offers a wide range of books and educational materials. Weather permitting, St. Helens may be seen 30

Mount St. Helens Visitor Center at Silver Lake

Forest Learning Center, one of several interesting visitor centers on the
Spirit Lake Memorial Highway

miles to the east. A short, graveled walk winds around the building.
Summer hours are 9:00 A.M. to 5:00 P.M.; winter hours vary, so check
ahead of time. The center is open year-round except on Thanksgiving
and Christmas.

Hoffstadt Bluff Visitor Center. At 26 miles east of I-5, this facility offers food services, a gift shop, restrooms, and helicopter flights
to the mountain. It is managed jointly by Cowlitz County and the
Washington State Department of Transportation.

Forest Learning Center. Seven miles east of Hoffstadt Bluffs
Visitor Center is an interesting facility with exhibits presented by a part-
nership of Weyerhaeuser, Washington State, and the Rocky Mountain
Elk Foundation. The first exhibit is a complete forest ecosystem. Other
exhibits depict salvage logging and forest replanting. A small theater
shows a video of the eruption and damage to forests and property.
Outside a nature trail leads through young forest, and observation areas at the bluff's edge provide views of the valley bottom far below. Elk
are almost always in sight, so be sure to have your binoculars in hand.
The hillside across the highway was near the edge of the blast zone,
and all the 90-foot trees were blown down there. They were ultimately
salvage logged, the area was replanted, and it is thriving today.

Coldwater Ridge Visitor Center. Highway 504 descends from
its high point at Elk Rock to the visitor center at 3,080 feet elevation

600 feet above Coldwater Lake. Opened in 1993, the center has a cafeteria, gift shop, computerized interpretive exhibits, and a small theater showing a film depicting the area's story and explaining the area's rebirth and renewal. Outside the center, the exhibits and short trail are barrier-free.

A wide, outside deck provides panoramic views that sweep from Minnie Peak at the head of the lake, past high peaks of the Mount Margaret area, to St. Helens, which rises 7 miles away above an ocean of hummocks and the Pumice Plain. Coldwater Lake, 3 miles long, was created by blockage of a stream valley on May 18, 1980. The lake is now 200 feet deep and covers a formerly forested valley. The ridges on both sides of the lake were heavily logged before the eruption, and whatever forest was there was blown down. A scenic trail follows the west shore of the lake, and another climbs for miles on the ridge across the lake.

A few yards west of the visitor center is the barrier-free Winds of Change Trail. The Elk Bench Trail begins 100 yards east of the center and drops steeply 1 mile to the lakeshore. From the deck you can see the Coldwater Lake Recreation Area at the foot of the lake.

Johnston Ridge Observatory (JRO). The 8-mile drive to the JRO from Coldwater Ridge takes you past the Coldwater Lake Recreation Area and the parking lot for the Hummocks Trail, a unique 2.3-mile trail through a wilderness of landslide hummocks with streams, ponds, and wonderful views. The trailhead for the Boundary Trail, which climbs for miles up Johnston Ridge, is located at the Hummocks Trail parking area.

From the large parking area, the unique observatory is reached by a 100-yard barrier-free walk. The JRO has been built into the hillside to minimize its impact on the natural scene. The view is, of course, magnificent with the mountain only 5 miles to the south. The viewing deck virtually hangs over the hummocks and area of total destruction.

Johnston Ridge is named in memory of David Johnston, a volcanologist who died on this ridge during the 1980 eruption. He was thought to be in a safe location for monitoring the mountain's activities. His last radio message was, "Vancouver. Vancouver. This is it!"

▪ HOW TO USE THIS BOOK ▪

This book describes the area's most scenic spots for people interested in any or all of the activities described below. Hiking is the monument's most popular outdoor recreation, and trails have been designed for this purpose. The trail descriptions herein are thus largely for hikers, but information about other recreation, where applicable, is given in detail. Several of the trail descriptions are exclusively for cross-country skiers or climbers.

The introduction to each chapter gives the lay of the land and general and scenic driving directions. Information about particular recreation opportunities in the vicinity are provided in the introduction if those activities are not covered in the trail descriptions themselves. Each trail description begins with a capsule description; icons that designate the type of activity appropriate to the trail (activities are described below with their appropriate icons); the length and difficulty of the hike; the types of users found on the trail; elevation gain; what maps to use; and the best season to visit. Driving directions to each trailhead are also provided.

Activities

The monument offers a wealth of activities for every type of visitor. Beginning in 1997, as part of a three-year pilot program authorized by Congress, fees will be charged for use of certain faciltities, including visitor centers, Windy Ridge Viewpoint, Ape Cave, backcountry developed campsites, and selected trails and recreation sites. Three-day or annual passes ($8 and $24, respectively; discounts are available for seniors) may be purchased at visitor centers, Windy Ridge, and at several businesses in Randle, Cougar, Toutle, and Castle Rock.

Because this is a monument and not a national park, hunting is allowed in all but one area: the Loowit Corridor. Exercise caution at all times, especially during elk season in the fall.

Driving Tours. The introductions to each of the four sections of this book include driving directions for scenic routes to each part of the monument. The most heavily used road in the monument is State Highway 504, which leaves I-5 and goes 52 miles east to its end in the heart of the blast zone at the Johnston Ridge Observatory. In winter this highway is open as far as the Coldwater Lake Recreation Area 2 miles beyond the visitor center.

All other roads within the monument are Forest Service roads. They are identified in this guide with the initials FR (forest road). The main FRs are identified by two-digit numbers and are usually paved two-lane or one-lane routes with turnouts. Roads with four digits are secondary routes whose gravel surfaces are usually well maintained. Roads with three digits and signs placed away from junctions are not suitable for passenger cars. Roads marked with $2^1/2$-inch green reflector circles are open for recreation. Roads not marked with these reflectors are not open to recreational use and are closed for wildlife management and protection.

Hiking. The Forest Service has created an excellent trail system in the monument. There is probably more contrast in trail types here than in any other hiking area of the Northwest, with routes across shadeless desertlike expanses, steep hillsides of loose pumice and ash, and dense, cool forests. Although some trails are suitable for novice hikers, many sections of trail are placed on steep hillsides, which makes for difficult walking but stunning views.

Most areas of the monument have fragile, soft soils and surfaces that are easily damaged. Restrictions are being eliminated on some trails, so some movement off-trail is possible—but not encouraged. You will find that using a trail is always more efficient. With washouts, drifting, and luxuriant plant life, a trail is occasionally difficult to follow. If you find yourself off the trail, stop, think, and return to where you last saw it. Make short probes in different directions. If there are elk tracks, follow them; elk like to follow trails and may give you a clue. Whenever you are off-trail, be careful and cause as little damage as possible.

Serious hiking on any trail anywhere in the monument should be done in hiking boots, not in sandals, tennis shoes, or jogging shoes. Steep canyon walls require boot soles that edge and hold and do not roll and slip. Synthetic or wool socks are the most comfortable, and a thin inner sock should also be worn to absorb the friction of walking. Cotton socks should never be worn for hiking as they are abrasive when damp.

Backpacking. The best opportunities for backpacking are to be found in the Mount Margaret Backcountry, the Green River valley, and the area to the north including the Goat Creek and Goat Mountain Trails. The monument plans to limit the number of backcountry hikers and require permits for entry into backcountry camps.

The Mount Margaret Backcountry (MMBC) has the only developed campsites with toilets and tent pads in the Monument. Reservations for these campsites are being considered, although unreserved use may be available for 1998 . Camping in the MMBC is restricted to eight developed sites, and tents must be on tent pads for resource protection. When MMBC campsite construction is completed, there will be room for only 44 campers. A daily per-person fee will be charged. Backpackers should contact the Monument prior to entering the MMBC to verify regulations. Dispersed camping is allowed in the northern Monument, the Mount Venus area, and along the Loowit Trail.

Mountain Biking. Many trails are open in the monument to bikers. Many are challenging—steep, narrow, exposed to long dropoffs, crossing rugged lava flows, or having soft ash and pumice treads. If a described trail in this book is open to mountain biking it is

Uprooted and broken trees on Crescent Ridge, west side of Mount St. Helens

so indicated with an icon and noted in the trail's information block (under "Users"). Where mountain biking is favorable, a description of the specific terrain for bikers is given at the end of the general trail description.

Mountain bikers should know how to prepare for a backcountry riding trip. They should keep in mind the safety considerations given at the end of this chapter and remember that special clothing and equipment are necessary when hitting bike trails. (An excellent guide that gives all such information is Tom Kirkendall's *Mountain Bike Adventures in Washington's South Cascades*, also published by The Mountaineers.) Bikers should be especially sensitive to hikers on multiple-use trails and never venture into areas of the monument in which mountain bikes are not permitted.

Cross-country Skiing. The chapters in this book about the south, west, and east sides of the mountain discuss in some detail the skiing possibilities to be found in the monument and contain several trail descriptions exclusively for skiers.

The best cross-country skiing in the monument—and some of the most scenic in the Northwest—is found on the south side of the mountain. There are two Sno-Parks on the mountain's south face, and although they are at low elevations (2,350 and 2,650 feet), there is usually adequate snow depth with a normal Cascades November-through-April ski season. Skiing on the east and west sides of the monument is more limited, and there are few marked trails. There is no skiing on the north side of the mountain. Skiing on monument trails near Coldwater

Ridge and Coldwater Lake is permitted but not recommended as most trails are steep, lead into avalanche-prone areas, and off-trail travel is prohibited.

Heavy snowmobile use on some roads requires skiers to use caution. For up-to-date information on snowline elevation and snow and road conditions, call the Mount St. Helens Ranger District in Amboy, Washington.

For complete information on how to prepare for a cross-country ski trip, including equipment and safety considerations, see my *Cross-country Ski Routes, Oregon*, 2nd edition, published by The Mountaineers. This book includes many ski tours in the monument.

Climbing. The south side of Mount St. Helens was reopened to climbing in 1987. As of early 1997, the following regulations were in effect, subject to future change: Climbing permits are required year-round and limited to 100 per day; permits for weekends are often reserved months ahead. A single-use climbing permit is $15; an annual permit is $30. There are no senior or children's discounts.

Advance reservations are available by mail or in person at the monument headquarters. Forty unreserved permits are assigned daily on a first-come, first-served basis at Jack's Restaurant & Store on Highway 503 about 23 miles east of I-5 and 5 miles west of Cougar. At 5:30 P.M. a roster is made for those seeking permits for the following day, and at 6:00 P.M. a lottery assigns names by random selection. Permits are for one person only and are valid for 24 hours starting at midnight. Being on the 5:30 P.M. roster does not guarantee a permit if more than 40 have signed up. Group permits are available. All travel above 4,800 feet on St. Helens requires a permit for each person in all seasons.

Most climbers use snowshoes or skis and carry gear suitable for climbing, such as crampons and ice axes for hard or icy surfaces. Winter climbers usually drive to Marble Mountain Sno-Park (2,650 feet, Sno-Park permit required) and go up the Swift Creek Ski Trail, continuing at the end of the marked trail straight up open slopes, across to the west side of Swift Creek, and up increasingly steeper slopes on lava flows to eventually merge with the summer Monitor Ridge route.

If you plan to climb the volcano, you must possess adequate physical skills and proper equipment before heading up. You should be especially careful when walking out onto the cornices on the summit rim. The prevailing winds are from the south, and they blow snow over the edge of the crater rim along the entire south side, creating unstable, unsupported ledges.

Caving. The south side of St. Helens boasts Ape Cave, the longest lava tube in the world. Visitors to the cave should dress appropriately and carry two sources of light. See trail description 17.

Horseback Riding. There are several trails in the monument suitable for horseback riding. These trail descriptions are noted with icons and described in the text.

Wheelchair Access. Most of the wheelchair-accessible trails in the monument are close to the visitor centers. Trails suitable for wheelchair users are discussed in the introduction to each section or marked with icons and featured in the trail descriptions.

Difficulty Ratings

Determining trail difficulty involves more than just steepness and length, though these are basic criteria. Factors such as the type of trail, obstacles, and ease of routefinding are also considered.

Easy. Generally level, gentle rolling, or gentle uphill grades to 6% (6 feet rise per 100 feet horizontal distance), up to a total distance of 6 miles.

Moderate. Usually gentle rolling to climbing with grades 7% to 12%, up to a total distance of 10 miles.

Difficult. Some demanding grades, 12% to 16%, some rough trail tread or obstacles, up to a total distance of 12 miles.

Very Difficult. Rough trail tread, obstacles, some steep grades over 16%, distance 15 miles or over; some routefinding may be involved.

Maps

The maps in this book are based on the author's personal experience with the trails. For convenience in descriptions, these maps may use site names not shown on official maps. Maps in this guide often illustrate several trails to encourage loop hikes and identification with the region and its other opportunities. Mileages and elevations may not always be in exact agreement with other maps but are reliable. Always carry other maps to supplement the book's maps and to make your hikes more meaningful.

The Mount St. Helens National Volcanic Monument map (scale 1:63,360), published by the U.S. Forest Service, is the single best map of the monument and is the map recommended for hikers. This ranger district map (called "brown line topographic") covers the entire monument and shows 40-foot contours in a rust color with a scale of 1 inch per mile. It shows almost all the trails accurately. However, Trails 184B, 205, 213B, 218, 237, and a short section of Trail 211 in the Mount

Margaret Backcountry are not shown. This map complements this guidebook's maps, which in many cases provide additional detail. The cover of this map has a rust-colored waterfall photo: Do not confuse it with other attractive maps in multi-colors that do not show all the trails.

The Gifford Pinchot National Forest visitor map (scale 1:126,720) has easy-to-read representations of roads. It also has a matrix listing recreation sites and opportunities, and a wide range of forest information.

Green Trails maps (scale 1:69,500) are the most useful maps for hiking in the monument but do not cover the entire area. The trails are shown with green lines, hence the name, are updated periodically, and are very accurate. They are commercially published and widely sold in outdoor stores and visitor centers. They are printed in multiple colors, easy to read, and have 80-foot contours, which are adequate for all trail hiking here.

United States Geological Survey (USGS) quadrangle maps of the 7.5-minute series (scale 1:24,000) are excellent topographic maps

A Weyerhaeuser logging truck destroyed by the 1980 flood in North Fork Toutle River

with remarkable detail at 2.64 inches per mile. This scale, however, is not necessary for hiking within the monument. Do not be deceived by the stream lines—the porous soils quickly absorb most water. The disadvantage of USGS maps is that they show few of the forest roads and often do not show recently constructed trails.

▪ WHAT TO TAKE ▪

All cross-country travelers should prepare thoroughly for trips into the outdoors, taking into account their own skill levels. Hikers, bikers, skiers, and climbers should know how to use a map and compass for navigation and should carry the ten essentials:

1. Map
2. Compass
3. Flashlight with extra bulbs and batteries
4. Extra food and water
5. Extra clothing
6. First-aid kit
7. Matches or lighter in a waterproof container
8. Pocket knife
9. Fire starter (to get wet wood to start burning)
10. Sunglasses

Because of the special conditions in the monument, travelers should consider taking along the clothing and equipment described below. Depending on the activities you decide to engage in while at the monument, you will need additional specialized gear and skills. You must know how to prepare for your outdoor sport before heading into the monument.

Walking Aids. To make your hiking safer, a walking staff or ski poles with baskets removed (so they don't hang up on vegetation and limbs) may be helpful. Even experienced hikers find that descending steep canyon sidewalls can be intimidating and dangerous. A walking aid will give you a third point of contact and help in climbing or crossing steep slopes and in maneuvering across deadfalls (rotted, blown-down trees).

Sun Protection. Because much of the monument is without shade, sunblock should be applied. Long-sleeve shirts and a sunhat should be worn. If it is hot, wear short pants but carry lightweight, long pants for afternoons. Cotton garden gloves will protect your hands in warm weather and are cooler than synthetic ones. Light, clear industrial goggles are useful when dust is blowing.

Rain Gear. Windproof clothing and wet-weather gear are recommended as the weather will not always be clear and hot. Weather in summer and fall may include periods of cool or cold temperatures, so carry clothing for a wide range of weather.

Water. Normal precautions should be taken when drinking water found in the monument. However, drinking water is scarce throughout the monument as the porous, volcanic soils absorb water quickly and there is rarely a reliable source. Most trails are "dry," so one should always carry water. Water is usually found at campsites, where its source is sometimes melting snowbanks, which means there will be none in late summer. One quart per day is the minimum to carry. In hot weather you should carry—and drink—two to three quarts per day.

▪ A NOTE ABOUT SAFETY ▪

Safety is an important concern in all outdoor activities. No guidebook can alert you to every hazard or anticipate the limitations of every reader. Therefore, the descriptions of roads, trails, routes, and natural features in this book are not representations that a particular place or excursion will be safe for your party. When you follow any of the routes described in this book, you assume responsibility for your own safety. Under normal conditions, such excursions require the usual attention to traffic, road and trail conditions, weather, terrain, the capabilities of your party, and other factors. Because many of the lands in this book are subject to development and/or change of ownership, conditions may have changed since this book was written that make your use of some of these routes unwise. Always check for current conditions, obey posted private property signs, and avoid confrontations with property owners or managers. Keeping informed on current conditions and exercising common sense are the keys to a safe, enjoyable outing.

—The Mountaineers

Mount St. Helens West

Boundary Trail near Johnston Ridge Observatory with view of the Pumice Plain and crater of Mount St. Helens

■ ■

On the west side of the monument the landscapes and the mountain with its enormous, yawning crater are the focus of interest. The drive into the west side is particularly scenic, and numerous viewpoints and educational facilities are found along the way. The Spirit Lake Memorial Highway, State Highway 504, carries some 2 million visitors annually into the monument. This modern highway climbs to 3,800 feet and ends in the monument. As there are neither campgrounds nor overnight facilities, visitors must return on it.

■ ACCESS ■

From Seattle/Tacoma. Drive I-5 south to Exit 63, drive through Toledo on Highway 505 to the junction with Highway 504, the Spirit Lake Memorial Highway, which takes you into the monument. This route bypasses one of the visitor centers. To get to the Mount St. Helens Visitor Center, take I-5 south to Exit 49 at Castle Rock and drive 5 miles east on Highway 504, the principal access route into the monument.

From Portland. Drive I-5 north 49 miles from the Columbia River bridge at Vancouver to Exit 49. Turn right onto Highway 504. From I-5 at Exit 49, it is 5 miles to the Mount St. Helens Visitor Center, operated by the U.S. Forest Service and a "must" stop.

Farther along the highway are two more visitor centers, each an interesting stop. The large Coldwater Ridge Visitor Center is 43 miles from I-5, and 8 miles farther at 4,200 feet is the end of the highway

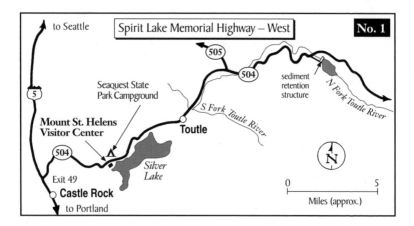

and the last visitor center, Johnston Ridge Observatory, which is also closest to St. Helens. These last two are within the monument and are operated by the U.S. Forest Service.

Driving Tour

Of the three principal routes into the monument, Highway 504 is the most traveled, starting at I-5 and extending into the heart of the volcanic zone. It ends high on a ridge 52 miles from the freeway. In winter, the highway is open only to the Coldwater Lake Recreation Area 2 miles beyond the Coldwater Ridge Visitor Center.

This spectacularly scenic highway was opened in 1993 after years of construction. The former highway along the North Fork Toutle River to Spirit Lake was almost totally destroyed by the mudflows of the eruption, which extended some 70 miles to the Columbia River. The road had followed the river closely and was washed out for many miles and in some places buried under 500 feet of debris. The present highway has been located higher up on the sides of the valley, resulting in much open, scenic viewing.

■ RECREATION OPPORTUNITIES ■
Wheelchair-accessible Hikes

There are many wonderful hiking trails on this side of the monument, described in detail in the complete trail descriptions. The following two very short trails, easily accessible at the Coldwater Ridge Visitor Center, showcase the natural history of the area.

Winds of Change Trail. This barrier-free, 400-yard trail starts near the west wing of the visitor center and leads through an area devastated by the 1980 eruption. Interpretive signs describe volcanic forces and the regeneration of plant life. Study plots are maintained along the trail and used as part of a curriculum for thousands of students who

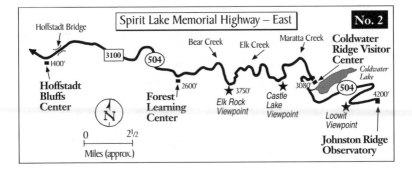

View from Castle Lake Viewpoint on Spirit Lake Memorial Highway of the North Fork Toutle River valley

visit the monument on environmental and science education projects. Walk the trail counterclockwise, and take binoculars and camera to record the exceptional views.

Birth of a Lake Trail. Enjoy a barrier-free boardwalk from the picnic area that takes you out over Coldwater Lake. There interpretive signs describe the creation of the lake. As a result of the eruption landslide that blocked the valley, this lake slowly formed behind a debris dam. The lake's present level is 200 feet above the former valley. Within five years of the lake's formation, complete aquatic communities had formed naturally.

Cross-country Skiing

This side of the monument is unfortunately not a skier's paradise, although the views are wonderful. There are no Sno-Parks along Highway 504, but wide turnouts are plowed near Elk Rock, about 6 miles from the visitor center. West of Elk Rock at milepost 33.5 near Bear Creek is Weyerhaeuser Road 3340, which leads up to other roads for skiing in the Elk Rock area. Between Elk Rock and the visitor center it is possible to ski on open slopes above the highway to a nearby ridgetop road that travels along miles of scenic skiing on gentle grades. This area is not in the monument but offers the best skiing and viewing. At Elk Creek, 1.2 miles east of the Elk Rock viewpoint (3,750 feet), parking and uphill access to the ridgetop are possible.

Highway 504 beyond the Coldwater Ridge Visitor Center (3,080 feet) is plowed in winter only to Coldwater Lake. If you park along Highway 504, be sure you are off the highway and legally parked or you may be cited. Skiing is not allowed in the area around the visitor center. Snow depth is not always dependable in this area. Call the visitor center for snow conditions.

Backpacking

The area north of Snow Lake is little visited by hikers. There are no trails at this time, and its remoteness from the trailheads discourages exploration. The area includes Mount Venus and four lakes: Venus, Lower Venus, Island, and O'Conner. The lakes lie in deep basins enclosed by steep ridges. Winding through the area are transitions from blow-down forest to standing dead forest and to green forest at the fringes of the 1980 lateral blast.

Venus and Lower Venus Lakes are in standing dead or "ghost" forest. Island and O'Conner Lakes are in the green forest, just a few hundred yards from the fringe. Mount Venus deflected the blast and protected forest to the north, although trees on the southern slopes were killed by the extreme heat.

Camping is not allowed at Venus or Lower Venus Lakes. Dispersed camping is allowed in the green forest, although an area on Island Lake's south shore is closed to camping to allow fragile lakeshore vegetation to recover from past impacts.

■ ■

1. Lakes Trail 211

Lakeshore trail traveling through wildflower fields with grand views

🚶🚶 🚶

Length ■ End of lake 3 miles, end of trail at Bear Pass 13 miles
Difficulty ■ Moderate to end of lake, Difficult beyond
Users ■ Hikers, Backpackers
Elevation ■ Trailhead 2,490 feet
Cumulative Gain ■ 500 feet in 6 miles
Maps ■ (Maps 3, 5, 21), Green Trails 332 (partial coverage), USGS Spirit Lake West

Season ▪ March through October
Driving Directions ▪ From Coldwater Ridge Visitor Center drive
    Highway 504 2.2 miles toward Johnston Ridge Observatory; take
    side road to lake recreation area and the trailhead at boat launch.

Skirting along the west shore of Coldwater Lake, the Lakes Trail offers a pleasant hike as it rolls along, gently gaining and losing height.
Although the Elk Bench Trail, starting at the visitor center 600 feet
above, connects with this trail, the boat launch trailhead is the recommended start. The trail derives its name from its use as access to the
high lakes near Mount Margaret, but those lakes are best reached from
Norway and Bear Passes. This trail is also less suitable as access to
Coldwater Peak than the South Coldwater Trail, which is shorter.

    From the boat launch hike north. Reach a junction at 0.7 mile with
the Elk Bench Trail. Just beyond are toilets. If you hike down to the
lake on the Elk Bench Trail, you will have to make a long climb to return. Beyond the junction, the trail continues rambling north through
wildflower fields. In side draws where there are small streams, alders
have grown quickly into tunnels of greenery that provide delightfully
cool temperatures on hot days.

    As you hike the trail you will notice many stumps where pre-

View from Coldwater Ridge Visitor Center across Coldwater Lake and the
Coldwater Lake Recreation Area

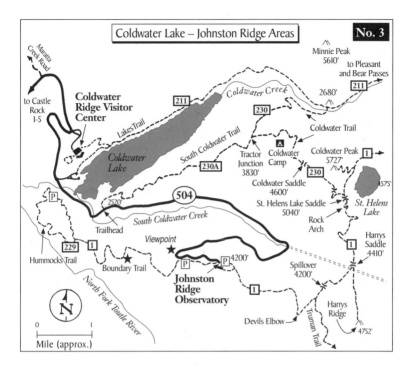

eruption logging occurred, and in other areas you will see blow-down forest. The blow-down areas—with uprooted trees, a chaos of roots, and tree trunks lying in different directions—are curious. With its wide-spread greenery and lush growth, it is hard to envision this valley after the 1980 eruption with a heavy layer of gray ash and debris from the stone wind. (The eruption's pyroclastic flow included 500 miles-per-hour winds of gasses, steam, and air carrying an incredible load of pumice, ash, and stones of all sizes that caused great damage, stripped bark and limbs from trees, and blew trees down.)

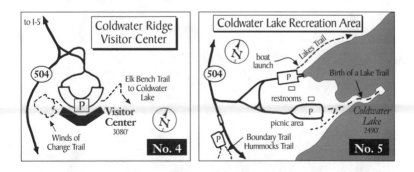

If you are an explorer and long-distance hiker you may want to continue beyond the end of the lake, hiking under Minnie Peak to the junction at 5.2 miles with Trail 230, which climbs to join the South Coldwater Trail. These trails permit a loop of 10.9 miles that returns down the ridge along the other side of the lake. A car shuttle or bike would help return 1.1 miles to the trailhead.

Backpacking. The easiest access for backpacking is from Lakes Trail 211. Near the intersection of Trail 211 and Whittier Trail 214 at Pleasant Pass (5,200 feet, 8.4 miles from the Lakes Trail trailhead at Coldwater Lake), follow good elk trails to the northwest. Gain the 5,360-foot saddle just south of Venus Lake, then drop about 400 feet to the lake and an additional 300 feet down to Lower Venus.

For more challenges, go up the ridge from the saddle just south of Venus Lake to the summit of Mount Venus. To reach Island Lake descend the northwest ridge to a saddle at 5,560 feet. There a descent of steep, forested, brushy and mossy slopes and cliffs leads to Island and O'Conner Lakes. Island Lake's south shore is closed to camping.

Hiking time to the summit of Mount Venus or Venus Lake is approximately 1½ hours one way and 2½ hours from the Lakes Trail to Island Lake. Snow Lake campsite provides a good base for explorations of this area.

If you are hiking the Lakes Trail to the backcountry, the developed campsite at Snow Lake (4,700 feet, 8.4 miles) is the first place to camp. The next camp is Shovel Lake, 1.3 miles farther. There is also a campsite on Trail 230 on the way to Coldwater Peak. See backcountry access information (Backpacking) on page 35.

Hikers on Lakes Trail, with Coldwater Lake and Minnie Peak in the distance

■■■■■■■■■■■■■■■■■■■■■■■■■■■■■■■■■■■■

2. Hummocks Trail 229

*A loop through hummocks and mini-canyons
with streams, ponds, and remarkable views*

🚶🚶

Length ■ 2.3 miles
Difficulty ■ Moderate
Users ■ Hikers
Elevation ■ 2,500 feet
Maps ■ (Map 6), USGS Spirit Lake West
Season ■ April through October
Driving Directions ■ From the Coldwater Lake Recreation Area
    drive 0.2 mile on Highway 504 to the trailhead parking area.

The Hummocks Trail is an unusual loop through a chaotic landscape:
giant piles of rocks, ash, and gravel of many colors are scattered about
randomly. The hummocks are up to 500 feet high and cover an area
that was once lush forest. The trail winds along with many ups and
downs along a seemingly aimless course. You will pass grassy meadows
surrounded by desolate piles of debris, green mini-valleys with micro

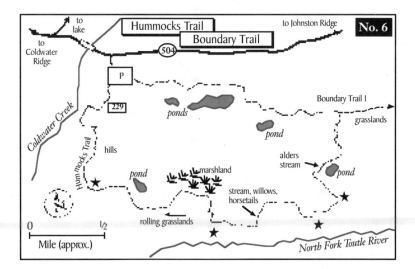

Hummocks Trail loop looking across hummock mounds to Mount St. Helens

streams, ponds surrounded by grasses and reeds, then reach a terrace-top viewpoint of the fast-moving South Fork Toutle River with its wide gravel flats and braided streams. Across are more hummocks, greatly eroded by the river. Mount St. Helens rises majestically in the distance.

The trail loops back to the parking area.

■■■

3. Boundary Trail I to Johnston Ridge

*An easy, long ridge climb, then a hike
through blow-down forest and wildflower fields*

Length ■ Loowit Viewpoint 4 miles, Johnston Ridge Observatory 4.8 miles, Truman Trail 7.3 miles
Difficulty ■ Moderate to JRO, Difficult to Truman Trail
Users ■ Hikers
Elevation ■ Trailhead 2,500 feet, JRO 4,200 feet, Truman Trail 4,020 feet

Maps ▪ (Maps 5, 7), Green Trails 332 (partial coverage), USGS
   Spirit Lake West
Season ▪ June through September
Driving Directions ▪ From Coldwater Lake Recreation Area drive
   0.2 mile to the parking area for the Hummocks Trail and the
   Boundary Trail.

The section of the Boundary Trail described here extends to St. Helens
Lake Saddle. There are three points of access to this section of the trail:
Hummocks Trail–Boundary Trail parking area, Loowit Viewpoint, and
Johnston Ridge Observatory.

The Boundary Trail extends some 60 miles eastward to Keenes
Horse Camp north of Mount Adams. The trail starts near Coldwater
Lake, climbs Johnston Ridge, and continues to circle St. Helens Lake,
passes near the summit of Mount Margaret, descends to Norway Pass,
then goes on to Bear Meadow. The trail leaves the monument near
here and goes east along high, rugged ridges of the Dark Divide to
end north of Mount Adams.

Trailhead to Loowit Viewpoint. Park at the Hummocks Trail parking
area. The Boundary Trail has a separate starting point at this parking
area, and its initial 0.8 mile passes through the hummocks area on a
route parallel to but out of sight of the Hummocks Trail loop. Once
beyond the Hummocks Trail area, it crosses a wide, flat, grassy basin
surrounded by hummocks.

Climb out of the basin at the foot of Johnston Ridge and cross another open area, a small but perfect example of an alluvial fan. Marked

Lupine flowers on Boundary Trail, one of many varieties growing profusely
in the pumice and ash of the blast zone areas

North Fork Toutle River valley from Hummocks Trail, looking southwest toward Castle Lake Ridge

by posts, the trail is on sandy deposits from the "stone wind." Now climb a rocky gully onto the foot of the ridge, passing a curious stepped, tan-colored rock dike, then lose the trail in an erosion gully in a chaos of washouts that feed the fan below. This example of erosion is typical of the unstable materials of much of the monument lands where trail washouts are common.

Climb the shallow gully, fed by a major ravine off the side of the ridge, 300 yards to its top through a thriving forest of tall alders. At the top is a spectacular scene: St. Helens above a sea of rugged hummocks, the North Fork Toutle River, and Castle Lake Ridge across the Pumice Plain. Hike across gravelly hummocks, turn left at a trail post, and climb across bleak, gray morainelike mounds onto the ridge. As you climb the dusty trail, note how your boot prints mix with those of resident elk.

Reach the ridge crest for fine views of the mountain and an aerial view of the hummocks and the roaring river. You will cross sandy, soft slopes. As you reach a sandy dome you may lose the trail, so look up and get your bearings. The highest, rounded point with standing dead trees is the point where you will circle below and around to the right.

Continue climbing and enter a blow-down where the trees conveniently form ash-filled ramps for the trail. Now heading toward the mountain the trail turns onto steep, grassy hillsides covered with lupine and dandelion. As you look down onto descending ridges and basins you are looking at a favorite elk grazing area. Pass under low rocky bluffs on a loose pumice tread where the trail is both drifted and washed out. As you pass "leaner" blow-down arranged at all angles on the steep slopes, you are close to the Loowit Viewpoint, 1,420 feet above your start.

Loowit Viewpoint to Johnston Ridge Observatory. As you look from the viewpoint to the mountain only 5 miles away, huge areas of hummocks lie below, with rugged, deeply eroded river canyons cutting through the jumble. It is hard to grasp that the great landslides climbed to within 100 feet of the viewpoint, then sloughed back down carrying huge volumes of debris to final rest on a bench far below. A trimline is easily seen to your left. You can see Loowit Falls tumbling 250 feet into a deep gorge across the way and above the Pumice Plain.

The trail leaves the east end of the viewpoint and traverses steep hillsides, then climbs along the ridge crest and eventually returns to the steep, south-facing slopes with the mountain always in view. Near the JRO it crosses green hillsides and then exits onto the highway near the parking lot to continue up the ridge from across the parking area.

Johnston Ridge Observatory to the Spillover. From the parking area it is a 100-yard walk on a barrier-free route to the JRO. From the east corner of the parking area the Boundary Trail goes 200 yards to where it is joined by Eruption Trail 201. This latter trail, although only 0.3-mile long, starts at the JRO and goes to an overlook, winds about the ridge, travels east along the barren ridge, then cuts back down to near the parking area, where it joins the Boundary Trail. The Eruption Trail was designed for visitors who want to sample trail walking and the desolate ridge still barren from the forces of the 1980 eruption.

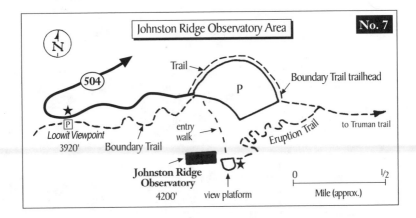

As you hike east on the Boundary Trail toward the Truman Trail, Coldwater Peak is the most prominent summit to the north. To its right is a rugged ridge with towers, the site of the natural rock arch through which the Boundary Trail crosses from one side of the ridge to the other. To the east, the closest ridge is Harry's Ridge, named for Harry Truman, who operated a resort and lived at Spirit Lake, where he died in the 1980 eruption.

As you proceed along the ridge, going over and around high points, you will have views of Mount Adams, Windy Ridge, then the long ridge that reaches from there up to the Plains of Abraham. As you get farther along, the trail takes a long swing around the south side of a prominent point on the ridge, and as you swing back around the far side you look up at the Spillover in a saddle beside Harry's Ridge. On the side of Harry's Ridge notice the trimline made by the great landslide as it glanced off the ridge on its way to climb, then cross, Johnston Ridge.

The last stretch to the junction with the Truman Trail will always have problems with erosion. At the junction you should push yourself to go the 400 yards to the Spillover saddle, a worthwhile extension. The trail up is rough and rocky and often hard to follow, but the views and the immediate area of the saddle with its chaos of hummocks are interesting. At the Spillover you must decide whether or not to go farther. To the top of Harry's Ridge is another 1.8 miles and an elevation gain of 550 feet. To the natural rock arch above St. Helens Lake is 2.2

Mount St. Helens viewed from the Boundary Trail near Loowit Viewpoint

miles and a gain of 900 feet, not including a side trip up Harry's Ridge.

Spillover to Harry's Ridge. From the Spillover saddle at 4,200 feet follow the trail along a 1.0-mile route up into a grassy basin where the trail traverses the wrinkled, open slopes logged many years ago. When you reach Harry's Saddle, a wide, sandy area at the head of the basin, note the thousands of elk tracks, a gathering place of elk herds, no doubt, and a ridge-crossing route for them. From the 4,410-foot saddle head south 0.8 mile up sandy slopes covered with greenery along an ill-defined route up the wide, rounded ridge crest. At the top stands a monitoring station, and the views are exceptional. Look down into Bear Cove, an arm of Spirit Lake, and then across the many miles of volcanic destruction.

Spillover to Natural Rock Arch and St. Helens Lake. Follow directions above to Harry's Saddle, then climb north out of the saddle onto the green hillside where the trail turns left on a long, climbing traverse that may be hard to locate due to growing plants. The trail eventually switches back and keeps climbing with improving views from the open hillsides. The trail goes around a sharp bend up high, goes west onto the ridge crest and onto its west side through dead forest. It then descends and switchbacks to a final short traverse through standing dead forest to the natural rock arch. You will see Mount Adams through the arch, and below is St. Helens Lake with its rafts of logs. The trail continues 360 yards along a rocky, exposed trail blasted out from an overhanging tower. It then drops to St. Helens Lake Saddle and the junction with the Coldwater Trail. It is a wild place with views of the rugged ridges and basins that drop to Spirit Lake from the Coldwater Peak/Dome Ridge.

■■■■■■■■■■■■■■■■■■■■■■■■■■■■■■■■■■■■■■■

4. South Coldwater Trail 230A

Exceptional views from an open ridge,
access to high-country trails and the Coldwater Peak summit

🚶🚶

Length ■ Coldwater Saddle 5 miles, St. Helens Lake Saddle 6.2 miles, Coldwater Peak 7.4 miles
Difficulty ■ Difficult
Users ■ Hikers

Elevation ■ Trailhead 2,520 feet, Coldwater Saddle 4,600 feet, St. Helens Lake Saddle 5,040 feet

Maps ■ (Map 5), Green Trails 332, USGS Spirit Lake West

Season ■ Late June through September

Driving Directions ■ From Coldwater Lake Recreation Area drive 1.1 miles on Highway 504 to the trailhead parking area.

Start on easy grades climbing a dry, west-facing hillside logged years before 1980. Large stumps with chewed surfaces attest to the power of the pyroclastic flow even behind Johnston Ridge. As the trail steepens, cross to the ridge's north side for views of the visitor center and the large delta at the foot of the lake.

Climb through thick alder and bright yellow wood groundsel flowers, then cross the ridge again for views down into the South Coldwater valley. At 1 mile hike into blow-down with views down the Toutle to Elk Rock and Spud Mountain to its left. Again, cross the ridge and reach a bluff edge with the lake far below and a first view of Minnie Peak at the lake's head.

Below is a logging company water truck with a blasted-out windshield and a cab filled with pyroclastic-flow debris. Then reach

Above: A Forest Service ranger stands beside the logging tractor blown from a high ridge on May 18, 1980.

Opposite: Boundary Trail on Johnston Ridge with view of the Pumice Plain and crater of Mount St. Helens

a battered yarding machine partially buried with debris. Look nearby for the yarding mast, a 60-foot steel tube of ¹/₄-inch steel crumpled in half. A short distance farther is a bulldozer half-buried and filled with wood and debris.

Next, follow an old road so covered and drifted with debris that it is aesthetically acceptable for a wilderness trail. Climb a bit, then drop over a distance to Tractor Junction where Trail 230 climbs up out of the valley to St. Helens Lake Saddle. Near the junction is a large, up-ended tractor, half-buried, blown off the high ridge above and tumbled down to this permanent resting place as a testament to the power of unleashed nature.

After 3.5 miles, this may be the place for some hikers to turn around, but there are a lot of rewards for continuing. To complete a loop, hike down to the Lakes Trail and back along the lakeshore, a total of 10.9 miles with 1.1 miles left to complete the hike along Highway 504. Better yet, continue climbing another 1.5 miles to Coldwater Saddle along a spectacular, steep mountainside where the trail is virtually a ledge. The views become exceptional with wild ridges and steep mountainsides dropping precipitously into the deep Coldwater Creek valley.

Shortly above Tractor Junction pass a small cirque at 4,000 feet where Camp 8 of the backcountry is sited with tent pads and a fly-in, fly-out toilet. There are fine views of Minnie Peak and Mount Whittier from near the cirque. Climb around a steep corner onto an airy ridge crest—now you find you are on a real mountain. Continue to obvious and large Coldwater Saddle at 4,600 feet, where you can rest and admire the views north to St. Helens and down to the Spillover and Johnston Ridge. Behind is Minnie, and Venus partly seared and partly green, the edge of the death zone, and Pleasant Pass above Snow Lake and at the foot of Mount Whittier.

Continue by climbing and crossing great grassy hillsides 0.9 mile to a small notch at 5,200 feet, then drop to nearby St. Helens Lake Saddle for the view of the lake below. To the right, up the Boundary Trail 360 yards, crossing an airy trail blasted out from under an overhang, is the natural rock arch the trail actually passes through, and a view of Adams.

At 5,727 feet, Coldwater Peak is the fifth highest of the backcountry peaks. From St. Helens Lake Saddle it is 1.2 miles and an additional gain of 700 feet to the top and site of a former fire lookout, now occupied by a seismic relay station. This route from the trailhead is the shortest one to the top of Coldwater Peak.

Mount St. Helens East

Heated water from the crater plunges 250 feet over Loowit Falls here on a side trail from the Loowit Trail.

■ ■

Windy Ridge (Map 8) with its many viewpoints and short trails attracts thousands of tourists every month of its short season, June through October, and its many long trails make it a natural destination for hikers. The great attractions here are Mount St. Helens itself, the area of total destruction below and north of its huge crater, and Spirit Lake and the miles of devastation that surround it.

The eastside approach from FR 25 offers ten points of interest along the 16-mile route that winds a sinuous course along the south side of Windy Ridge to its end at the viewpoint. These include other viewpoints, especially Cedar Creek, Donnybrook, and Windy Ridge. The viewpoints at Independence Pass, Harmony, and Windy Ridge also offer hiking trails.

For hikers interested in the Loowit Trail, please refer to the St. Helens South chapter, where all sections of the trail are described.

■ ACCESS ■

From Seattle/Tacoma. Drive I-5 south and in Tacoma take Exit 133. Drive Highway 7 to Morton, 90 miles from Seattle. At Morton drive east 17 miles on Highway 12 to Randle, then south 20 miles on

From a ridge high above St. Helens Lake near the rock arch. Spirit Lake and Truman Ridge are in the center, and Spillover Saddle is on the right.

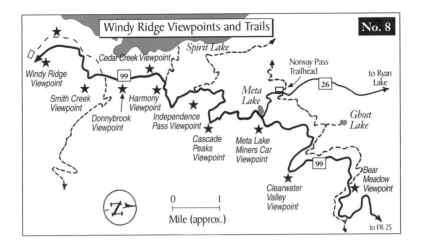

FR 25 to FR 99. Drive FR 99 4.7 miles to Bear Meadow Viewpoint, then into the monument and onto Windy Ridge with its several trailheads and outstanding viewpoints of Spirit Lake and St. Helens. The end of Windy Ridge is 16.4 miles from the junction of FR 99 and FR 25. From Seattle, Windy Ridge is 142 miles, or 182 miles if I-5 is driven to Highway 12. In winter, FR 25 is plowed only to FR 99 and the Wakepish (WAKE-eh-pish) Sno-Park, 20 miles south of Randle.

From Portland. There are two routes from Portland to the junction of FR 25 and FR 99. The shortest is 109 miles, via Cougar then FR 90 to FR 25, and the longer is 143 miles via I-5 and Highway 12 to Randle, then south on FR 25.

Driving Tours

There are two scenic drives to the east side of the monument, coming from the north through Randle or south through Carson.

From the north to Windy Ridge. The majority of eastside visitors to Windy Ridge come through Randle on Highway 12 and drive the 20 miles south on FR 25 to reach FR 99, the Windy Ridge Road. After leaving Randle, drive south and in 1 mile keep right onto FR 25. At 5.7 miles reach the Woods Creek Information Center. Across the road is a picnic area and the Woods Creek Watchable Wildlife Interpretive Trail, composed of two loops with a total walking distance of 3 miles.

Three miles beyond the information center is the junction with FR 26, severely damaged in February 1996 by washouts and landslides. Initially believed irreparable, it may be reopened by 1997. In another mile arrive at the USFS Iron Creek Campground located in a grove of ancient trees, the closest camping to the monument. You may choose to park at the Iron Creek Picnic Area just south of the campground entrance to walk the wonderful 1.5-mile trail that circles the campground.

As you continue your drive on FR 25 you will pass FR 2516, which climbs 6 miles to the Strawberry Mountain Trail. Continue up FR 25 to Iron Creek Falls, only a 500-foot walk to the 40-foot falls spilling from a lava overhang. At FR 99 turn west to enter the monument.

From Carson to Windy Ridge. From Carson at the Columbia River, follow the Wind River Highway (FR 30). At 12 miles from Carson pass the USFS Beaver Campground. At 14 miles pass a turnoff to the trailhead for Falls Creek Falls, where the trail climbs along a beautiful route to the high falls. Cross Old Man Pass at 3,000 feet and 24 miles from Cougar, then go 2.8 miles to FR 51, which proceeds downhill 7 miles to FR 90. Then drive 5.4 miles west on FR 90 to FR 25, which is followed north to Windy Ridge.

A Forest Service Information Center on FR 25 is 0.2 mile south of the junction of FR 25 and 90. Drive north on FR 25 0.7 mile and stop at the wayside exhibit to look at the Pine Creek boulder, a 37-ton boulder lifted 30 feet onto the highway by the May 18, 1980 mudflow. Drive 3 miles to the Cedar Flats Nature Trail, a 1-mile loop through majestic old-growth cedar forest. Continue 11 miles to a viewpoint of St. Helens and the Clearwater Valley, a wide, deep U-shaped valley carved by a glacier 12,000 years ago. Cross Elk Pass at 4,080 feet and descend to FR 99, which leads to Windy Ridge.

Natural rock arch where Boundary Trail passes through to nearby St. Helens Lake

Once on FR 99, you will climb steadily through mature green forest almost 5 miles to Bear Meadow, where you first glimpse St. Helens, 11 miles away. The road then descends, winding in and out of side valleys to the Clearwater Valley Viewpoint at the edge of the blast zone, where tall, bleached dead trees stand in the scorched zone next to green forest.

At 4.5 miles from Bear Meadow, both FR 26 and Meta (MEE-tah) Lake are reached. FR 26, which goes north to the Ryan Lake area and back to Randle, was so severely damaged in 1996 by road washouts and landslides that it may be 1997 or 1998 before it is reopened. The short barrier-free trail at Meta Lake exhibits the survival of trees, animal, and plant life, protected from the 1980 eruption by a deep layer of snow and the high neighboring ridge.

Farther along the road at Cascade Peaks Viewpoint, Mounts Adams, Hood, and St. Helens can be seen and the only food service facility on Windy Ridge can be found. Independence Pass Viewpoint is next with a 300-yard walk through blown-down trees to a good view of Spirit Lake. A short walk farther up the trail improves the view dramatically, and an even longer walk is recommended to a viewpoint high above the lake at 1.7 miles. Harmony Viewpoint, 8.8 miles from Bear Meadow, has a 1.5-mile trail to the shoreline of the lake, the only access to Spirit Lake in the monument. The hike is scenic and descends along the wall of a glacial cirque formed 12,000 years ago.

The next two nearby viewpoints, Cedar Creek and Donnybrook, have perhaps the best views on Windy Ridge, except at the top of the stairs at Windy Ridge Viewpoint at the end of the road. At Smith Creek Viewpoint, farther along, the view south into the deep, U-shaped glacial valley is impressive. A 9-mile trail goes down the valley. There is an excellent view of St. Helens here, the best view from the Windy Ridge road. The mountain is seen rising above a deep valley and rugged foreground ridges.

Windy Ridge Viewpoint has a fine view of St. Helens, the Pumice Plain at its foot, and of the west end of Spirit Lake with Johnston Ridge rising beyond. The stairs rising behind the restrooms replace the former "sand ladder" made of dowels and cables and give access to an upper trail that goes through blow-down forest on a barren ridge to a nearby viewpoint, a 15-minute walk, where a panoramic view of the entire region may be enjoyed. The trail, a short extension of the Independence Pass Trail, continues along the ridgetop. Then it drops off onto the ridge's west face on an airy route that ends at the Smith Creek trailhead on the Windy Ridge road, 1.4 miles from where it started at Windy Ridge Viewpoint. The monument hopes to complete the missing section to

Floating log masses and Mount Adams seen from above Truman Saddle on Boundary Trail looking down to Spirit Lake

Independence Pass, about 2.8 miles away, which will result in a trail extending from Norway Pass along the full length of Windy Ridge.

▪ RECREATION OPPORTUNITIES ▪

Cross-country Skiing

The east side of the monument south of Randle has only the Wakepish Sno-Park at the junction of FR 25 and FR 99 (2,800 feet). At this time, there are no marked ski trails and it is almost 5 miles up FR 99 to a view of St. Helens at Bear Meadow. It is possible to ski up FR 25 and several other forest roads in the area, but you will find little variety and few rewards. One possible pleasure is the old-growth forest (see Bear Meadow to Elk Pass description). However, the most scenic tour at this time is to drive then ski up FR 2516 to wonderful views of Adams and Rainier from the ridge north of Strawberry Mountain (see Strawberry Mountain description).

Backpacking

The backcountry surrounding Mount Margaret is the premier backpacking area of the monument with its numerous lakes, peaks of all shapes, high ridges, and rugged, scenic trails. To experience this area of imposing cliffs, ancient glacial cirques, and exceptional views requires an investment of three days or more. There is a daily limit on the number of overnight backpackers allowed in this area. Call the monument headquarters in Amboy for information on permits. If your time is limited, the long, one-day round-trip hike to the top of Mount Margaret will give you an overview of what the small range of peaks has to offer.

It is a compact area of rugged ridges, deep valleys, and lake basins extending roughly east to west some 7 miles from Bear Pass to west of Coldwater Peak. The small range is located from 6 to 10 miles northeast of St. Helens. There are nine major peaks, of which Mount Whittier is the highest and Mount Margaret is the second highest with an easily climbed summit requiring no special skills. Coldwater Peak, the fifth highest and in an isolated location to the west, can be easily ascended by trail.

The Norway Pass Trail is the most popular access route serving the Boundary Trail as well as connecting with the Lakes Trail and going through from east to west.

■■■■■■■■■■■■■■■■■■■■■■■■■■■■■■■■■■■■

5. Boundary Trail I:
BEAR MEADOW TO ELK PASS
An easy walk through exceptional old-growth forest

🚶🚶

Length ■ To Elk Pass 4.8 miles, or short 1-mile hike
Difficulty ■ Easy
Users ■ Hikers
Elevation ■ Bear Meadow 4,097 feet, Elk Pass 4,090 feet
Maps ■ (Map 9), Green Trails 332, USGS Spirit Lake East
Season ■ Late June through September
Driving Directions ■ Drive to junction of FR 25 and FR 99, then drive FR 99 4.7 miles to Bear Meadow Trailhead, or 3.6 miles to the lower trailhead, which is 1.1 miles below Bear Meadow.

The trail starts just east of the restrooms at Bear Meadow Viewpoint and descends 1.3 miles on gentle grades through lovely but unremarkable

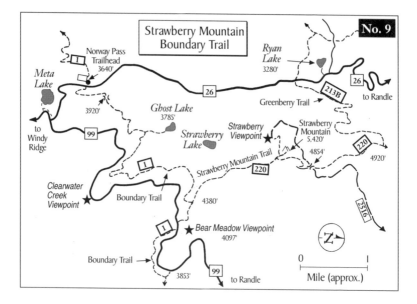

forest to where it rejoins FR 99. For lovers of old growth, this lower trailhead is where to start hiking. The trail is suited to casual walkers who want a brief exposure to ancient forest, and to more serious hikers who want to explore farther.

The trail from the lower trailhead at first climbs along the side of a low ridge where a thick understory of young trees crowds the big ones. Once up this grade the trail levels out, rolling along where a smooth, carpetlike forest floor replaces the crowded small trees. This is pristine, classic old growth that offers quiet and isolation away from the busy road.

An abandoned logging road crosses the trail 0.5 mile from the start. If it is followed to the west uphill 500 yards past a recuperating clearcut, a view of St. Helens may be had. After this detour return the same way back to the trail, which soon starts a long, gentle descent beside a shallow gully through more scenic forest. After a mile a clearcut on the left is buffered by mature forest, then the trail starts climbing onto a low ridge. About 0.5 mile before reaching Elk Pass on FR 25 you come out into an old clearcut on the edge of a ridge with a view of Strawberry Mountain and Mount Rainier.

The Boundary Trail crosses the road at FR 25 and continues about 30 miles east to near Mount Adams. From Bear Meadow, the Boundary Trail goes to the Coldwater Lake area about 25 miles to the west.

■ ■

6. Boundary Trail I:
BEAR MEADOW TO GHOST LAKE
TO NORWAY PASS TRAILHEAD

*Introductory hike through lateral blast, green forest,
scorched zone, blow-downs, Ghost Lake*

🚶🚶

Length ■ From Bear Meadow 6 miles, 1.5-mile short introductory
   hike to Ghost Lake
Difficulty ■ Moderate for regular trail, Easy for short hike
Users ■ Hikers
Elevation ■ Bear Meadow 4,097 feet, Norway Pass Trailhead 3,640
   feet at FR 26
Maps ■ (Map 9), Green Trails 332, USGS Spirit Lake East
Season ■ Late June through September
Driving Directions ■ Drive to junction of FR 25 and FR 99, then
   drive FR 99 4.7 miles to Bear Meadow Viewpoint and the trailhead.

Cross the road at Bear Meadow to the trailhead and hike 200 yards for
a good view of St. Helens, which is better than the view at the viewpoint itself. Then enter old growth and climb steeply to a junction with
the Strawberry Mountain Trail 0.6 mile from Bear Meadow. Turn left

On the Boundary Trail to Ghost Lake where the green forest changes to
standing dead trees of the scorched zone. FR 99 is below.

and follow a rolling trail along a steep hillside with several screened views, then out of the old growth into a forest where standing dead trees mingle with living, green forest. This is the transition zone where the pyroclastic flow and stone wind lost much of their destructive power, yet there was still sufficient heat to scorch and kill healthy, big trees. Descend the trail and see broken trees, then blow-down forest. Descend farther into a shallow valley where many trees lie in a chaotic jumble, the result of a large blow-down of green trees in the storms of February 1996.

Near here the side trail to Ghost Lake goes north 0.4 mile to the small lake surrounded by standing dead forest. After leaving the lake, near the jumble of downed trees, follow the trail up a long climbing traverse, then switchbacks ascending to a hillside above a lovely, open basin surrounded by standing dead forest. Bismark Mountain stands directly above. When you reach the low pass, you will be just 0.8 mile from the end of your hike, the Norway Pass trailhead, which you will be able to see.

Short Hike. Start your hike at the Norway Pass trailhead, cross the road, and—slightly north—find the trail that leads to the low pass on the Boundary Trail to Ghost Lake. This scenic, short hike is a good introduction to the eruption forces and how it affected the forests. You will see tall, green trees protected by ridges; standing dead, broken forest; and blown-down trees.

■■■■■■■■■■■■■■■■■■■■■■■■■■■■■■■■■■■■■

7. Strawberry Mountain Trail 220

The most easily reached high point in the monument, with views from a former fire lookout site

🚶 🎿

Length ■ North side short trail 0.7 mile, from Bear Meadow 2.5 miles

Difficulty ■ Short trail Moderate, Long trail Difficult

Users ■ Hikers, Skiers

Elevation ■ Trailhead on short trail 4,854 feet, Bear Meadow trailhead 4,097 feet, high point 5,466 feet

Family picnic on top of Strawberry Mountain, site of a former fire lookout

Maps ■ (Map 9), Green Trails 332, USGS Spirit Lake East
Season ■ Late June through September
Driving Directions ■ For the hike from Bear Meadow Viewpoint, drive to junction of FR 25 and FR 99, then drive 4.7 miles on FR 99 to trailhead; for the short hike, from Randle drive 18.2 miles on FR 25 to FR 2516, then drive FR 2516 uphill on good gravel surface 6 miles to parking area. (FR 2516 is 1.8 miles north and downhill from the junction of FR 25 and 99.)

The longer, southside approach to the summit travels through beautiful old growth, then onto an open ridge with views. From Bear Meadow Viewpoint cross the road and hike up the Boundary Trail. In 200 yards enjoy a view of St. Helens superior to that from the viewpoint itself. Enter forest and climb steeply 0.6 mile to the junction with Strawberry Mountain Trail. Do not go left but continue climbing on an unrelenting grade, still in old growth. At 1.3 miles the angle eases off as the trail rolls along the steep sidehill with screened views of Adams and Goat Rocks. Soon a small saddle appears just above the trail with a view west, but continue to the close-by saddle where the trail switches to the west side of the ridge.

Step out to grand views that improve as you climb the steep trail 800 yards through beautiful flower fields to an upper saddle (the saddle at which the short route ends). Then it is 50 yards to the ugly, abandoned logging road, then up and around a stump to the 150-yard trail to the summit.

Short Hike. From the parking area at a narrow pass on FR 2516, hike 150 yards south and uphill to the trail sign, then cut back and climb into the forest. Climb through old growth on a moderately steep tread to a saddle on the south ridge crest. A huge clearcut is below on the west side. Turn right and climb 50 yards to the end of an ugly,

abandoned logging road, then climb around a large stump to the final
150-yard trail to the top.

The view is stunning, with Rainier, Goat Rocks (a small, rugged
range north of Adams), then Adams, and farther south the Indian
Heaven high country, then Mount Hood. Mount St. Helens and the
Mount Margaret Backcountry peaks are directly across the deep Green
River valley. Margaret is on the left, and Mount Whittier with its three
rock towers is in the center. To its right is Pleasant Pass, the deeper of
two notches, then Mount Venus in the transition zone between scorched
forest and green forest. Goat Mountain, a long ridge, partly clearcut
and with both green forest and dead trees, rises above the north side of
the Green River valley as it turns west. There was widespread blow-
down in the Green River valley, and it was all salvage-logged within
two years.

Cross-country Skiing. The best opportunity for skiing on this side
of the mountain is FR 2516 (see Driving Directions above). Although
there is no Sno-Park here at 2,682 feet, the turnout is often plowed.
Otherwise, drive as far as possible up the maintained, gravel road, then
ski through clearcuts and second growth to a saddle at 4,255 feet, about
4 miles from FR 25 where there is a view of Mount Rainier. Continue
up the road and enjoy increasingly good views of Mount Adams. Ski
to the obvious saddle in a deep notch 6 miles from FR 25, then continue westward, if conditions are safe, across a very steep north-facing
hillside. The road circles around to the west side of the ridge for impressive views of St. Helens, the Mount Margaret range, and Goat
Mountain, the long ridge to the right across from Mount Margaret.

■■■■■■■■■■■■■■■■■■■■■■■■■■■■■■■■■

8. Independence Pass and Ridge Trails 227 and 227A

Hike through dead, blow-down forest with sweeping views

🚶🚶

Length ■ To Norway Pass 3.5 miles, loop distances up to 7.4 miles
from Independence Pass
Difficulty ■ Moderate
Users ■ Hikers

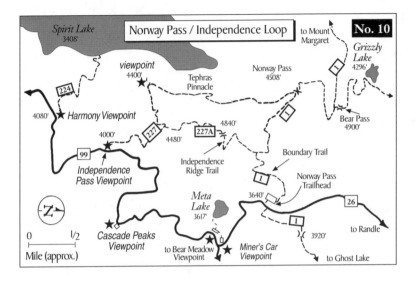

Elevation ▪ Viewpoint 4,000 feet, Norway Pass 4,508 feet, Norway Pass Trailhead 3,640 feet

Cumulative Gain ▪ From Norway Pass trailhead loop, 1,600 feet; from Independence Pass Viewpoint loop, 1,400 feet

Maps ▪ (Map 10), Green Trails 332, USGS Spirit Lake East

Season ▪ Late June through September

Driving Directions ▪ Drive to junction of FR 25 and FR 99, then drive 12.2 miles on FR 99 onto Windy Ridge to Independence Pass Viewpoint.

The Independence Pass Trail will be extended in the future along Windy Ridge to reach Windy Ridge Viewpoint. A section is now completed from Windy Ridge Viewpoint to the saddle at the Smith Creek trailhead.

Beginning at Independence Pass Viewpoint, this is one of the most scenic trails in the monument. Through blow-down forest are views of Adams, Hood, St. Helens, and Spirit Lake. To best appreciate the scenery of this section of Windy Ridge, make a loop trip that adds little distance compared to the out-and-back distance. Hike counterclockwise regardless of whether you start at the Norway Pass trailhead or Independence Pass Viewpoint. This direction ensures the most dramatic viewing of the area's major features.

From Independence Pass Viewpoint. Hike 300 yards through massive blow-down for a view of St. Helens and the lake, then continue up the

Grizzly Lake in a cliff-bound cirque on Lakes Trail 211

Camp I between Bear Pass and Mount Margaret, a developed backcountry campsite in an ash-filled saddle

ridge for views of Adams and Hood. Then turn a switchback and cross the dry, hot hillside to level trail where washouts from storms have damaged the trail. Drop quickly into the mouth of a small side valley, Harmony Creek, down which trail 227A comes to join your trail. Decide here if you have time for the 7-mile loop; if not, at least hike to the exceptional viewpoint 1.7 miles from the trail's start and now only 0.7 mile away. For the viewpoint, continue on the trail—not up the side valley, which is the loop route—round a shoulder of the ridge, and drop to an obvious rounded knoll 50 yards off the trail. Walk out onto the viewpoint and look down 1,000 feet at logs floating on the lake, then enjoy the sweeping scene from Norway Pass to your right to St. Helens.

If you are hiking the loop, however, save this knoll-top view for the last leg, and from the junction with 227A hike into the little side valley into a desolate scene of ash, uprooted trees, and many snapped-off broken snags. The raw look of destruction is eased a bit by small conifers and returning vegetation. The trail climbs gently out of the narrow valley onto a wrinkled sidehill and finally gains a saddle at 4,840 feet. The views of Rainier, Strawberry Mountain, and the Green River valley improve just below the saddle. Descend the trail to its junction with the Boundary Trail and follow it up to Norway Pass.

At the pass go left, climb 300 yards to a great view of the lake, then keep going on west-facing slopes with dramatic views of prominent buttresses descending to the lake. Drop to an ash-filled saddle, then down and across very steep slopes where there was much trail damage in 1996. Pass Tephra's Pinnacle, a 70-foot tower, and continue across steep, intimidating slopes to the knoll-top viewpoint. Then climb a bit to the small side valley, across the dry face, and down to the parking area where you started.

From Norway Pass Trailhead. The first leg of the loop goes to Norway Pass, then as on the other loop, along the scenic, wild, west-facing slopes of Windy Ridge to the knoll-top viewpoint, around the ridge's bulge to the small side valley, and up the valley to the saddle. Take time to enjoy the views, then hike down to the junction and back down to the Norway Pass trailhead to complete a slightly longer loop with only 200 feet more of elevation gain.

9. Harmony Trail 224

A scenic, interesting descent and the only trail to the Spirit Lake shoreline

Length ▪ Round-trip 3 miles
Difficulty ▪ Easy
Users ▪ Hikers
Elevation ▪ Trailhead 4,000 feet, Spirit Lake 3,400 feet
Maps ▪ (Map 10), Green Trails 332, USGS Spirit Lake East
Season ▪ Late June through September
Driving Directions ▪ Drive to junction of FR 25 and FR 99, then drive FR 99 13.5 miles onto Windy Ridge to the Harmony Viewpoint.

This heavily used trail offers interesting scenery, a profusion of returning plant life, the shoreline of Spirit Lake with views of St. Helens and its crater, exposure to blow-down forest and the giant wave that swept high into this small basin, and several features not seen on other trails.

There are often ranger-led hikes with lectures on the history of the eruption and its effects on this basin. Descend the trail as it hugs the steep sides of a cirque formed by an immense glacier over 12,000 years ago. The great landslide avalanche of 1980 crashed into the lake and created an enormous wave that flooded this basin and scraped all soil, vegetation, and forest on its walls to 500 feet above the present level of the lake, now 200 feet higher at its surface than prior to the eruption. This scraped area extends up to the "trimline," the upper edge of the wave's effect. The basin was filled with giant old-growth trees that were all swept away in moments.

Hike past the small gorge where Harmony Creek and Falls flow and picture a glacier 1,000 feet thick, grinding the exposed rock you see into smooth forms by its tremendous weight and the abrasive nature of the rocks and gravel under it. Turn the trail and note a smooth bench on the uphill side of the trail. Stop and examine this rock and note the striations and grooves from the glacier's passage. Where the trail turns again, walk on the glacially polished, rounded, and scratched rock.

Near the lake, look at St. Helens's crater and see the great snow-fields on the dome. With binoculars you might see wisps of steam. What appears as smoke rising above the crater's walls is usually dust created by the continuous rockfalls within the crater. The crater, rim to rim, is 1.25 miles across and 2,000 feet deep. Over the years the dome, now almost 1,000 feet high, will eventually become the new, higher summit of St. Helens.

Mount St. Helens seen across Spirit Lake from the beach at the end of the Harmony Trail

■■■■■■■■■■■■■■■■■■■■■■■■■■■■■■■■■■

10. Truman 207, Abraham 216D, and Windy 216E Trails:
PLAINS OF ABRAHAM
FROM WINDY RIDGE VIEWPOINT
*Superb views of St. Helens from high, green alpine trails
to desertlike pumice plains*

🚶🚶 🚲

Length ■ Plains of Abraham 4 miles, loop total 9 miles
Difficulty ■ Difficult
Users ■ Hikers, Mountain bikers
Elevation ■ Windy Ridge Viewpoint 4,200 feet, Plains of Abraham
    4,460 feet, Windy Pass 4,885 feet
Maps ■ (Map 11), Green Trails 364S, USGS Mount St. Helens
Season ■ Late June through September
Driving Directions ■ Drive to junction of FR 25 and FR 99, then
    drive FR 99 16.4 miles to end of Windy Ridge.

At the Windy Ridge Viewpoint go to the south end of the parking area,
go around a locked gate, and follow a former logging road around the
south shoulder of Windy Ridge 1.7 miles to the wide Truman-Abraham
Saddle. The road continues downhill as the Truman Trail onto the
Pumice Plain, to the Windy Trail, and to Johnston Ridge and farther.
At the wide saddle, the Abraham Trail leaves the Truman Trail and
climbs onto a narrow ridge. Follow the narrow crest 400 yards to a
saddle with great views of Adams and down into upper Smith Creek,
within a great U-shaped glacial valley. Here a 168-step sand ladder
makes climbing the soft pumice of the steep ridge easy. Continue across
the ridge's face to another sand ladder and back to the ridge crest. The
ridge is an ancient glacial moraine now covered with pumice.

   A ragged, wild ridge to the east descends from the Plains of
Abraham area. Yet higher see Rainier and the Goat Rocks. A mile from
the start of the trail at the saddle leave the moraine and start a sidehill
climbing traverse to the Plains. Cross numerous gullies filled with exceptional wildflower fields, then descend with your first view of the

A pleistocene-age glacier carved grooves into these rocks.

Plains and cross a black stone-filled wash to smooth pumice slopes. In 0.4 mile reach the junction with the Loowit Trail, 4 miles from the Windy Ridge parking lot.

If you are returning the way you came, hiking a bit south to explore the Plains and to get a feel for their size and isolation at the very foot of St. Helens. The Plains slopes rise smoothly onto the mountain's east side. The great, vertical slot in a rock wall at the head of Ape Canyon can be seen by walking south 1.5 miles across the Plains.

A loop return takes you over Windy Pass on the Loowit Trail, then the Windy Trail to the Truman Trail adds only 600 feet of elevation gain and a mile more to your return. If this is your choice, head up the Loowit Trail, cross several wide, dry washes along the trail marked by cairns carefully built of black rocks. It is a grind getting to the pass as you struggle up a loose, sand- and pumice-covered steep trail on Windy Peak's lower slopes. At the pass greet a strong breeze and enjoy the marvelous views across the Pumice Plain to Johnston Ridge. Descend 0.4 mile reach the junction with the Loowit Trail, 4 miles from the Windy Ridge parking lot.

Join the Windy Trail and follow it as it circles into the wide basin created by years of erosion from floods and melting snow. Climb above

large fields of lupine flowers to the Truman-Abraham Saddle and follow the road back to your starting point. This road was built for use by
the crews that pumped water from Spirit Lake to stabilize its elevation
and during the construction of the drainage tunnel under Harry's and
Johnston Ridges that carries water into the South Coldwater valley.

Mountain Biking. The Truman Trail is open to bikers as far as
the Truman-Abraham Saddle, an easy ride on a scenic, wide road. Then
the bike route continues up the Abraham Trail to the Plains of Abraham.
The Abraham Trail is steep, soft, and not rideable uphill. This trail is
for iron men and iron women prepared to push a lot, then carry their
bikes up two long sand ladders. Short sections on the ridge crest down
low are rideable, as is the top area, which is almost level. The Plains of
Abraham are open to bikers, as is the Ape Canyon Trail. One way,
Windy Saddle to the Muddy River Lahar, allows a 13-mile ride. A long
car shuttle is possible. See trail description 36 (Smith Creek Trail) for
car shuttle information.

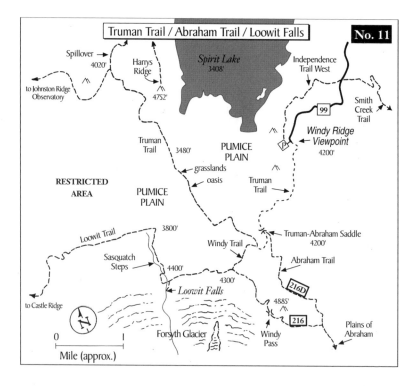

■ ■

11. Truman Trail 207:
PUMICE PLAIN TO JOHNSTON RIDGE
Volcanic deserts, a green oasis,
and a climb through landslide hummocks to the Spillover

🚶🚶

Length ■ To Spillover saddle 5.8 miles
Difficulty ■ Difficult
Users ■ Hikers
Elevation ■ Trailhead 4,200 feet, low point 3,480 feet, Spillover
saddle 4,200 feet
Cumulative Gain ■ Approximately 1,800 feet
Maps ■ (Map 11), Green Trails 332, 364S, USGS Spirit Lake West
Season ■ Late June through September
Driving Directions ■ Directions for Abraham Trail (see trail descrip-
tion 10).

Start hiking from the south end of the Windy Ridge Viewpoint parking area on a gated, pre-eruption logging road and climb gently around
the south side of the final extension of Windy Ridge; at 1.7 miles reach
the Truman-Abraham Saddle where the Abraham Trail forks off to the
left and climbs a narrow ridge.

Continue downhill on the road to the flats where the road turns
northward. Badly eroded in places, the road curves past low lava cliffs
and passes a stream. The road, no longer maintained, was used to haul
rafts, diesel engines, pumps, and other equipment used to temporarily
control the level of Spirit Lake and to dig a tunnel 11 feet in diameter
and 8,500 feet long to drain overflow water into South Coldwater
Creek. As the trail descends gently, arrive at a green oasis with streams
and dense stands of willows.

For the first time see Windy Ridge Viewpoint and the crater dome.
Reach another unique research area where an unusual grassland of tall,
red-stemmed grasses thrives and provides a home for insects and small
mammals. Soon cross a wide, sandy wash, then two more wide, rocky
washes where there is an undependable flow of water in August. The
trail continues to be marked with tall posts and cairns.

By now you have traveled almost 5 miles. Ahead is an area that ramps up to the Spillover on Johnston Ridge. Machine-worked surfaces are where spoils from the tunnel-drilling operation were discarded. As you start uphill the trail wanders about and disappears at times due to erosion and rocky surfaces. Walk across unusual, large areas of white, pure, fine ash, past mini-gorges and two small lakes, one muddy and one green. Large hummocks are scattered everywhere and scattered rocks, debris, and boulders litter the trail. It's a wild, desolate scene with almost no vegetation.

After a climb of more than 500 feet from the low point, arrive at the junction with the Boundary Trail that continues 2.5 miles west to the Johnston Ridge Observatory. Then travel uphill 400 yards on the difficult, rocky trail to the top of the Spillover, where a chaos of huge hummocks was left. This last mile of trail will always be badly eroded and hard to follow, although poles and cairns attempt to mark the route.

Along here enjoy a break. Take your binoculars and look at Loowit Falls plunging 250 feet into a deep gorge above the Pumice Plain, the large snowfields on the side of the dome, then the trimline on Harry's Ridge to your left. At the Spillover saddle look down into the South Coldwater valley to Highway 504 and the curve where the other end of the tunnel disgorges huge amounts of water all summer. If your desire here is to climb Harry's Ridge or up to the natural rock arch for a view of St. Helens Lake, refer to trail description 3 (the Johnston Ridge section of the Boundary Trail).

■■■■■■■■■■■■■■■■■■■■■■■■■■■■■■■■■■■■■■■

12. Boundary Trail I to Norway Pass

Loop trips through blow-down forest to Spirit Lake views and Mount Margaret summit

Length ■ Norway Pass 2.3 miles
Difficulty ■ Moderate
Users ■ Hikers
Elevation ■ Trailhead 3,640 feet, Norway Pass 4,508 feet, gain 900 feet
Maps ■ (Maps 10, 12), Green Trails 332, USGS Spirit Lake East

Season ▪ Late June through September

Driving Directions ▪ Drive to junction of FR 25 and FR 99, continuing 9.2 miles on FR 99 to FR 26, then north on FR 26 for 0.9 mile to the Norway Pass trailhead.

From the trailhead follow the trail up a low ridge. Then traverse the ridge southward, climbing steadily through blow-down forest to a junction with Independence Ridge Trail 227A at 1.3 miles. Continue on the Boundary Trail toward Norway Pass, round a ridge end from where you see the rest of the trail and the pass. Below is the Green River valley, a wide, U-shaped glacial valley carved out 12,000 years ago, with Rainier and the long ridge of Strawberry Mountain above. Across the way note the trail climbing eastward from Norway Pass up green slopes to Bear Pass, the lower of two saddles on the high ridge.

At the pass enjoy the view of Spirit Lake. If you are hiking only to the pass consider a short extension for even more dramatic views. Hike 300 yards up steep grades on the Independence Trail for views along the rugged west face of Windy Ridge, across which this trail continues to Independence Pass Viewpoint. Another side trip for grand views is a hike up toward Bear Pass on the trail to Mount Margaret, with a view in only 0.5 mile of Norway Pass with St. Helens and Spirit Lake beyond. Notice Adams 30 miles to the east and Hood 70 miles south. If you hike to Bear Pass, less than a mile above Norway Pass, you can look down into Grizzly Lake in its rock-walled cirque.

Lakes Trail between Grizzly Lake and Obscurity Lake, with blasted old-growth logs from 1980

At Norway Pass, don't be surprised to see hummingbirds buzzing in for a close inspection and white-throated swifts. Across the way on the trail to Bear Pass note the long white streak in a gully, which is a flow of pumice below a trail washout that required blasting a rock face above for a permanent, solid route. The pumice is from an ancient eruption.

Independence Trail Loop. Distance: 7.4 miles. Cumulative elevation gain: 1,600 feet from trailhead. Difficulty: Moderate. Route: Independence Trail 227, Independence Ridge Trail 227A, then Boundary Trail down to trailhead.

High Lakes Loop. Distance: 16.2 miles. Cumulative elevation gain: approximately 3,000 feet. Difficulty: Very difficult. Route: Bear Pass, Grizzly Lake, and other lakes via Lakes Trail 211 to Pleasant Pass, then Whittier Trail, Boundary Trail back to Norway Pass and to trailhead. Read trail description 15 (Whittier Trail).

Spirit Lake Loop. Distance: 24 miles. Cumulative elevation gain: approximately 4,300 feet. Difficulty: Very difficult. Route: Norway Pass, Mount Margaret, Boundary Trail around the Dome to St. Helens Lake, Truman Trail, Windy Pass Viewpoint, up stairs and trail to Smith Creek trailhead, hitchhike or bike to Independence Pass Viewpoint, then Trail 227, or 227A, to Boundary Trail and down to trailhead.

■ ■

13. Boundary Trail 1:
MOUNT MARGARET AND ST. HELENS LAKE

*To Mount Margaret summit and beyond on a scenic,
challenging ridge to the lake*

🚶🚶 🚶

Length ■ Mount Margaret 6 miles, St. Helens Lake 4 miles more
Difficulty ■ Difficult
Users ■ Hikers, Backpackers
Elevation ■ Trailhead 3,640 feet, summit high point 5,858 feet
Cumulative Gain ■ To summit 2,500 feet, to St. Helens Lake add 1,500 feet
Maps ■ (Maps 10, 12), Green Trails 332, USGS Spirit Lake East, Spirit Lake West

Trail junction above St. Helens Lake. The Dome is above the sign, and Mount Margaret is to the right.

Season ■ Late June through September
Driving Directions ■ See directions for Boundary Trail to Norway Pass (trail description 12).

This adventure takes you to the summit of Mount Margaret, second highest of the backcountry peaks, and encourages further exploration west along the spectacular ridge to St. Helens Lake and Coldwater Peak rising above the lake. Consider camping at Camp 1, the camp closest to the trailhead and Mount Margaret.

See the Boundary Trail to Norway Pass description (route 12) for the route to the pass. From Norway Pass, Mount Margaret is seen as an unassuming, almost flat-topped, serrated ridge with rounded rock peak to its right that appears higher.

From Norway Pass head for Bear Pass at 4,900 feet and on the way up look over your shoulder occasionally for exceptional views of St. Helens and Spirit Lake. Hike the 200-yard side trail to Bear Pass for the view of Grizzly Lake far below, the Green River valley and Rainier. Continue up the Boundary Trail for the rest of the day, and try to enjoy the unrelenting climb: It rewards you with endless green hillsides bedecked with myriad flowers of all colors.

In 1.5 miles from Bear Pass, reach Camp 1 at 5,500 feet, one of eight newly developed campsites in the Mount Margaret Backcountry. Camping elsewhere is not permitted. At the camp you will find tent pads that discourage needless disturbance of the fragile area, and a fly-in, fly-out toilet. Here you may find water from melting snow into late July, but don't count on it.

Continue climbing with continuous views of St. Helens and Spirit Lake and impressive, green hillsides, ridges, and rocky buttresses descending more than 2,000 feet to the lake. This is a truly dramatic area with constantly changing scenery. Descend into a saddle where the Whittier Trail starts, then continue across green slopes through alpine firs and descend into another sandy saddle with countless elk tracks. See the long, rugged crest of Whittier and admire the views. Climb only 300 yards to a shoulder where the trail splits (no sign) and take the trail to the right. In 300 yards the trail leads up sandy slopes to the base of the final, 25-foot, easily climbed rock tower of the summit. The view is magnificent.

Mount Margaret to St. Helens Lake. As you look westward along the long ridge to Coldwater Peak and ponder what lies ahead, think of it this way: The adventure has just begun. From Mount Margaret the trail drops 300 feet on several switchbacks to just the first of several saddles along the ridge. The route is too complex to describe in detail but is always obvious and often sandy, with many ups and downs. You

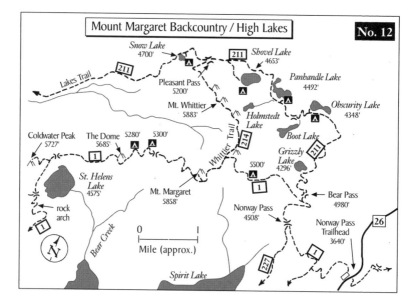

Abandoned monitoring site on side trail between Camps 2 and 3 on the Boundary Trail. The peak beyond is the Dome.

will pass two more developed campsites (Camps 2 and 3) and have an opportunity to take a side trip to a good viewpoint, all uphill. The trail then makes a long climb around the south side of the Dome, a prominent peak with a cliff-bound summit. Then descend into yet another saddle, followed by more descent to a high traverse around the north side of St. Helens Lake to the base of Coldwater Peak.

A steep switchbacking trail climbs to the top of Coldwater Peak, site of a former fire lookout that is now a volcano monitoring site with a seismic relay. The Boundary Trail now circles the west side of St. Helens Lake and reaches a saddle where Coldwater Trail 230 joins. This is another superb place, and you can make it even more interesting by hiking 360 yards farther uphill on the trail to several red rock towers where a narrow trail with vertical dropoffs has been blasted out of rock cliff. Stop in the shade of the natural rock arch where the trail actually goes through to the other side of the ridge for a great view of the lake and Adams here. The trail then climbs to a nearby ridge top, drops to join the Truman Trail, and continues on to the Johnston Ridge Observatory.

14. Lakes Trail 211 to the High Lakes

Rugged trail through blow-down to lakes in glacial basins

Length ■ From Norway Pass trailhead—Grizzly Lake 4.2 miles, Obscurity Lake 6.2 miles, Panhandle Lake 7.1 miles, Shovel Lake 9 miles, Pleasant Pass 8.8 miles, Snow Lake 9.3 miles
Difficulty ■ Moderate, to Pleasant Pass Difficult
Users ■ Hikers, Backpackers
Elevation ■ Trailhead 3,640 feet, Pleasant Pass 5,200 feet
Maps ■ (Maps 10, 12), Green Trails 332, USGS Spirit Lake East, Spirit Lake West
Season ■ Late June through September
Driving Directions ■ See directions for Boundary Trail 1 to Norway Pass (trail description 12).

The average hiker or backpacker is unlikely to hike the entire distance to Pleasant Pass in a day and is likely to camp at Obscurity (shown as Twin Lakes on some maps) or Panhandle Lake followed by a day trip or two.

From the pass hike the moderately steep trail to Bear Pass, enjoy the views, then descend almost 700 feet to Grizzly Lake in a rugged, small cirque. Camping is not allowed here.

Bridge near Obscurity Lake campsite on the Lakes Trail

A small segment of blow-down forest at Obscurity Lake in the Mount Margaret Backcountry

Continue on a rolling trail, often traversing steep hillsides with wide views of the upper Green River valley carved by glaciers. Elk herds are commonly seen below the trail. From Grizzly Lake, in 2 miles you will reach Obscurity Lake after a long haul up a shallow side valley into the lake's basin. The lake is surrounded by glacier-rounded hills with downed trees smothering the now-green slopes. It is a lovely, small basin and you may meet the resident great blue heron.

To reach Panhandle Lake, climb west over a 500-foot pass and descend to a side trail leading to the campsite on an alluvial fan. High ridges rise on the south side and culminate in cliff-bound lake cirques far up on the north side of Mount Whittier. Low, rounded hills on the lake's north side separate the lake from the Green River far below.

As you leave the lake, cross the outlet stream from Shovel Lake, which lies in a spectacular cirque above. Round the foot of a ridge, then start a grueling, steep climb with incredible views. As you climb higher you will enjoy beautiful vistas back over Panhandle and into Shovel Lake. You will also see Rainier, Goat Mountain, and Adams. Traverse a long hillside toward Pleasant Pass, bypassing a side trail that drops into Shovel Lake where another complete campsite is located. Snow Lake to the west sits just below the pass in a small, bleak basin.

At the pass, the Whittier Trail (which you should only attempt if you are an experienced backcountry hiker; see trail description 15) climbs steeply 300 yards to a snowfield, then continues very steeply, clinging to an intimidating cliffside.

An easier access route to Pleasant Pass starts at the Coldwater Lake area, which is the other end of the Lakes Trail you have been hiking on. Almost equidistant from Norway Pass, the west access on the Lakes Trail starts 1,000 feet lower and is less interesting.

■■■■■■■■■■■■■■■■■■■■■■■■■■■■■■■■■■■■■■

15. Whittier Trail 214:
MOUNT WHITTIER TRAVERSE
Very difficult cliffside trail passages,
extreme exposure to dropoffs, sweeping views

Length ■ 2 miles
Difficulty ■ Very difficult, dangerous for unskilled hikers
Users ■ Hikers with backcountry skills
Elevation ■ Low point Pleasant Pass 5,200 feet, Whittier summit 5,883 feet
Maps ■ (Map 12), Green Trails 332, USGS Spirit Lake East, Spirit Lake West
Season ■ Late June through September
Driving Directions ■ See directions for Boundary Trail 1 to Norway Pass (trail description 12).

Mount Whittier is the highest peak of the Mount Margaret Backcountry. It is a long, narrow, steep-sided ridge extending from Pleasant Pass to the Boundary Trail in a saddle northeast of Mount Margaret. The trail is a serious undertaking that traverses very steep terrain in places, both up and down. It skirts across the faces of cliffs and generally follows near or along the serrated crest of Whittier and crosses the summit. It is of equal difficulty whether you travel it west to east or the reverse. The average hiker will not be comfortable on this trail and may indeed feel it is dangerous. To hike this trail, you must have experience and confidence in your abilities to negotiate steep, difficult, off-trail travel. The direction of your traverse will depend on where you are camped since it can be done in a long loop from a camp at any of the lakes.

Opposite: Looking down from Shovel Lake to Panhandle Lake with its rafts of blasted, floating logs. Goat Mountain and Mount Adams are beyond.

On the summit crest of Mount Whittier, highest peak of the Mount Margaret Backcountry. Goat Mountain and Mount Adams are beyond.

There is little actual walking on the trail as you spend much time scrambling up and down steep slopes, looking for and finding the route, and using handholds. You will always be exposed to dropoffs.

The trail cannot be described piece by piece as it often changes course from one side of the ridge to the other, up, down, around obstacles, switching back, cresting, dropping into steep notches, then out and up the other side. The trail is usually visible, but if you don't pay careful attention you'll end up off route and will lose time.

From the southeast end near Mount Margaret the trail crosses a beautiful, green hillside facing west, goes along a rocky ridge, then passes three rock towers with very steep, short sections, both up and down, exposed to long dropoffs. Amazingly, one of the small, steep saddles here is a regular elk passage from one valley to another. Once around the towers, the long ridge awaits you. From Pleasant Pass the trail at first is deceptively normal though steep, then you are suddenly scrambling steeply along the face of a near-vertical cliff. When you finally swing around the end of a ridge you can breathe a sigh of relief. Now you can enjoy the splendid views without the distraction of your survival instinct. The views go on and on.

The Forest Service work crews who designed and built this trail, blasting it out in places, deserve a commendation for turning a daring concept into a unique experience. Like most trails in the monument, much of it is on sandy and pumice-covered areas where normal weather elements will cause some damage to the trail, covering and obscuring the route in places. The trail will not receive regular maintenance.

Mount St. Helens South

Old-growth forest on Toutle Trail south of Huckleberry Saddle

■ ■

The southern approaches to St. Helens lead to many superb trails. Trails here will take you through green forests; to the edge of stands where erect scorched trees died at the edge of the blast zone; through meadows; across hot, barren lava flows and a barren pumice desert; up to timberline areas where the famed Loowit Trail circles the mountain; to a small lake; to canyons, waterfalls, and roadside viewpoints; to a scenic horse trail; and even to a renowned lava cave 2 miles long. For variety, the south side of Mount St. Helens cannot be equaled.

In this guidebook, "south side" refers to all areas reached by the several roads that radiate from FR 81 and FR 83 on the mountain's south side and proceed either to the mountain's west or east side.

■ ACCESS ■

From Seattle/Tacoma. There are two routes to the village of Cougar on the mountain's south side: I-5 to Woodland Exit 21, then east on Highway 503; or to Tacoma, then Exit 133 to Highway 7 to Morton, east to Randle, and south on FR 25 to FR 90 to Cougar. The distance to Cougar is 174 miles via the I-5/Woodland route and 170 miles via the Morton-Randle route. If you drive the Morton-Randle route, on the way you can visit Windy Ridge and the southeast side of the mountain: Ape Canyon and the Lava Canyon trails, for example.

A shortcut on FR 2588 that usually opens in late June starts from FR 25, is most safely traveled by four-wheel-drive vehicles, but can be negotiated with great care by two-wheel-drive vehicles. It climbs 1,600 feet in 8 miles and offers no scenic rewards before reaching FR 83, but it is about 17 miles shorter to the Lahar-Lava Canyon area.

From Portland/Vancouver. There are two equally scenic routes that lead to all the trailheads on the south side of St. Helens. For most residents of the Portland/Vancouver area I-5 north to Woodland Exit 21 then east on Highway 503 will be the fastest route, although it is 5 miles longer than the alternative route. The I-205/Battleground/Amboy route also follows Highway 503, but on its southern extension. From the Columbia River it is 21 miles north to Woodland on I-5, then 23 miles east on Highway 503 to Jack's Corner, where Highway 503 turns south to Amboy and Battleground and enroute passes the headquarters compound of the Mount St. Helens National Volcanic Monument. From Jack's Corner it is 5.2 miles to Cougar (elevation 550 feet), a village where food and the last gasoline are available. This route to Cougar is also the route to the monument's east side and Windy Ridge.

If your interest is a trail on the west or southwest side of the mountain, turn off 1 mile before Cougar and drive north 11.3 miles on FR 81, past Merrill Lake to the junction of FR 81 and FR 8123 (elevation 2,700 feet). Refer to maps for your choice of roads from here to the nearby trailheads. FR 81 is at first two lanes and paved, then one lane paved with turnouts. Just before FR 8123 it becomes gravel.

If the south side is your goal, drive through Cougar on FR 90, two lanes paved, 6.9 miles to the junction of FR 90 and FR 83. FR 90 continues to the Lewis River valley , where it connects with FR 25 to Windy Ridge and Randle on Highway 12.

For southside trailheads turn onto FR 83 and drive 1.8 miles to the junction of FR 83 and FR 81 (elevation 2,350 feet). This junction gives access to the mountain's west and east sides. Your destination determines which way to go at this junction.

Alternative from Portland/Vancouver. From the Columbia River drive I-205 north 3.3 miles to Orchards Exit 30, then east on Highway 503, which soon turns north and passes Battleground in 9.7 more miles. Continue north on 503 through farm country on a hilly, winding two-lane paved surface. Drive through Amboy toward Jack's Corner 23.3 miles north of Battleground. Past Amboy 4.2 miles on the way to Jack's Corner, pass the headquarters offices and visitor information center for the monument. This is also your opportunity to purchase the USFS ranger district map of the monument; it will be your most useful possession for exploring the monument. This route to Jack's Corner is 5 miles shorter than the I-5/Woodland route but slower.

Note: FR 25 in winter is plowed only 20 miles south of Randle to the Wakepish Sno-Park at FR 99. From there southward to the Lewis River valley there is no winter snowplowing. From the south, FR 25 to Windy Ridge and Randle is normally not driveable until mid-June due to snow.

▪ RECREATION OPPORTUNITIES ▪
Cross-country Skiing

A wide range of opportunities awaits skiers on the south side of St. Helens above Cougar. There are short, easy loops in meadows, tours across lava flows, a small lake, and one-day trips to remote areas. There is no tour on this side of the mountain that does not have exceptional views, which is partly due to the extensive logging that took place many years ago.

16. Trail of Two Forests 233

Unique showcase of crumpled lava flow and wells

Length ▪ 400-yard barrier-free loop
Difficulty ▪ Easy
Users ▪ Hikers, Wheelchair users
Elevation ▪ 1,840 feet
Maps ▪ (Map 13), Green Trails 364, USGS Mt. Mitchell
Season ▪ June through October
Driving Directions ▪ Drive from Cougar 6.8 miles east on FR 90 to
the junction with FR 83, then 2 miles on FR 83 to FR 8303, then
west 0.2 mile on FR 8303 to the trailhead.

The name of this unusual exhibit, Trail of Two Forests, represents the
ancient burned forest and the regenerated forest now covering the area.
The entire trail is a nearly level barrier-free boardwalk with interpretive signs that explain features.

The most notable features are the buckled surface of the lava flow
and the tree molds left by trees up to 5 feet in diameter that were
engulfed by flowing lava 1,200 years ago. The trees burned and the
resulting molds left vertical wells up to 12 feet deep. Look into the wells
for bark impressions that formed on the hot lava. In one place a

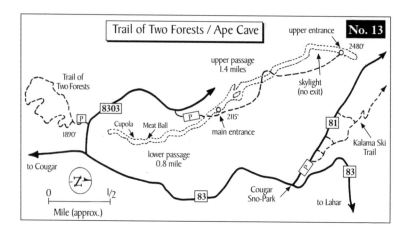

50-foot crawl-through of two connecting, horizontal, 3-feet-wide molds is an option for adventurers wearing old clothes and shoes. Each explorer should have a flashlight, but a headlight is preferred as you will be crawling on your hands and knees. A hard hat is a good idea, but a cap will give some protection from scratches. The crawl is reached via a 6-foot ladder in a tree well, and the nearby exit is marked for anxious family observers.

Please do not leave the boardwalk, and in the picnic area do not wander onto the nearby and fragile moss-covered areas.

17. Ape Cave Trail 239

Easily accessed and longest lava tube cave in the world

Length ■ Lower cave 0.8 mile, Upper cave 1.2 miles
Difficulty ■ Lower cave Easy, Upper cave Difficult
Users ■ Hikers, Cavers
Elevation ■ Entrance 2,115 feet, Upper exit/entrance 2,480 feet
Maps ■ (Map 13), Green Trails 364, USGS Mt. Mitchell
Season ■ June through October
Driving Directions ■ Follow directions for Trail of Two Forests, then drive 0.8 mile farther on FR 8303 to the trailhead parking lot.

This cave, the longest continuous lava tube in the world, was discovered in 1946. Today it is visited annually by over 80,000 people. It was formed 1,900 years ago when lava flowed down a streambed. Its top surface hardened into a crust while its liquid center continued to move. Eventually, the core lava flowed out at the bottom and left a cave behind.

Many visitors explore the cave with Forest Service ranger interpreters. In summer at the Ape Cave Headquarters building at the parking area, the Forest Service rents lanterns and conducts several talks and ranger-led tours daily. The cave is not lit, so carry two sources of light. Wear warm clothing as the cave remains about 42 degrees Fahrenheit year-round. A stairway gives access into the cave where long ago the roof collapsed and left a large hole on the surface.

The 12,810-foot cave is composed of an upper and a lower gallery

Main entrance to two-mile-long Ape Cave on the south side of Mount St. Helens

or tube. The lower cave, 0.8 mile long, is easier to walk as the floor is generally smooth and covered with sand. This section eventually narrows, and you must return the way you came. The cave varies in height and width and is over 40 feet wide and 20 feet high in some places. One of many distinctive formations is the "Meat Ball," where a large lava ball is wedged into a narrow overhead crevice.

The upper cave, 1.2 miles long, climbs 365 feet along a more interesting and demanding route to its exit. The cave twists about, widens and narrows, and in many places you have to climb over rough boulders and up steep, short sections. This makes it important to wear a headlight so you can use your hands. Unless you are a serious caver, you will probably not go farther than about 400 feet to the "Big Room." Above here the going gets rough with more obstructions to negotiate. The Big Room is 70 feet wide and 30 feet high and the floor is partially covered with lava boulders.

If you venture into the upper cave, note the walls and look for such markings left by the passage of hot lava as grooves, flutings, and deep gutters formed by subsequent, smaller lava flows. In fact, three lava flows are known to have descended through the cave, the most recent only 300 years ago.

If you climb through the cave to the upper exit, a trail back to the starting point leads through forest and across a boulder field left by floods.

■ ■

18. Goat Marsh Trail 237A

To a tranquil setting with views over a lake and marsh to St. Helens

Length ■ To marsh 0.9 mile, to viewpoint 0.3 mile farther
Difficulty ■ Easy
Users ■ Hikers, Mountain bikers
Elevation ■ Marsh 2,880 feet, elevation gain 60 feet
Maps ■ (Map 14), USGS Goat Mountain
Season ■ Late April through September
Driving Directions ■ Drive FR 81 to junction with FR 8123, then
north on 8123 0.6 mile to the small trailhead.

The marsh is a Research Natural Area with a grand view of St. Helens
across nearby Blue Lake. The lake and marsh, covering more than a
square mile, lie in a forested basin with the steep forests and cliffs of
Goat Mountain rising over 2,000 feet above.

From the trailhead hike downhill along a wide trail in the lodgepole forest (in winter, this is the Kalama Ski Trail) and turn right in 0.2

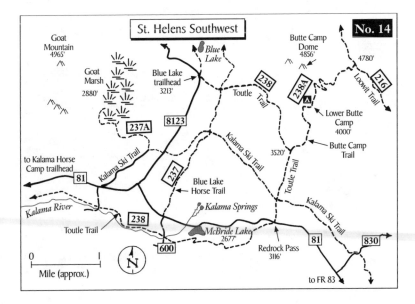

mile, hike uphill, pass through a gate, and enter beautiful big trees in a level setting for the remainder of the walk to the lake's shore.

For the best views of the lake and the marsh beyond, walk 100 yards beyond where you first arrived at the shore, enter some brush behind a small inlet, then work your way back to the shoreline in a few yards to the now obvious trail. Hike around the west shore to a point where you will see all of the lake and marsh. Below is a large tree that has been a longtime project for a beaver. Make your way down to a bleached log and sit on it to examine the beaver's work and enjoy the scene. Lily pads and marsh grasses make a nice foreground for a photograph of the mountain reflected in the lake.

Use your binoculars to examine the mountain and to look for wildlife. For more scenery, continue farther on the trail. Be prepared for mosquitoes here, or they will ruin your hike.

Mountain Biking. This is a short ride, but the trail is compact with few obstacles.

■ ■

19. Kalama Ski Trail 231

*11-mile trail starting at Cougar Sno-Park
and ending near Goat Marsh Trail*

Length ■ 4 miles to Redrock Pass, total 11 miles to end
Difficulty ■ Moderate
Users ■ Hikers, Skiers
Elevation ■ 2,350 at the Sno-Park 3,116 feet to Redrock Pass
Maps ■ (Maps 13, 14, 18), Green Trails 364, USGS Mount
    Mitchell, Mount St. Helens, Goat Mountain
Season ■ December to March
Driving Directions ■ Drive to the junction of FR 83 and 81, where
    Cougar Sno-Park is located

This ski trail climbs 4 miles on gentle to moderate grades from the
Sno-Park to Redrock Pass. It passes a rolling lava flow with a fine view
of St. Helens. From the pass, the trail continues northwest, climbing
through a mixed forest of fir and lodgepole pine, crossing the Blue Lake
Horse Trail, and descending to pass near Goat Marsh to end at the
Kalama Horse Trail near McBride Lake.

Starting at the Sno-Park, the trail to Redrock pass goes by three
short connector trails that form small loops for skiers looking for a casual experience. The trail then climbs through thick forest into old
clearcuts with scattered old-growth trees, then turns into wide, open
slopes of old clearcuts. This is a good place to ski off the trail onto the
lower slopes of Monitor Ridge. Back on the trail, it crosses FR 830,
which climbs high on the ridge from where there are sweeping views
of the region south of the mountain. From the FR 830 crossing the
trail continues on to the pass through alternating areas of forest and
open land.

Aggressive skiers may want to ski beyond the pass to the end of the
trail where FR 81 can be skied back to the Sno-Park for a 15-mile loop.

Opposite: Trailside maidenhair fern and fungi

20. Toutle Trail 238:

KALAMA RIVER TRAILHEAD TO REDROCK PASS

Through mixed forest following Kalama River to McBride Lake,
old growth, Redrock Pass

Length ▪ 5.6 miles
Difficulty ▪ Easy
Users ▪ Hikers, Mountain bikers, Horseback riders
Elevation ▪ Trailhead 2,070 feet, Redrock Pass 3,116 feet
Maps ▪ (Map 14), Green Trails 364, 364S (partial coverage), USGS
Goat Mountain, Mount St. Helens
Season ▪ Late April through September
Driving Directions ▪ West of Cougar 1 mile, drive FR 81 north past
Merrill Lake to the Kalama Horse Camp 8.4 miles from the start
of FR 81 on the Cougar highway

Toutle Trail is a gerrymandered product that goes east to Redrock Pass,
turns abruptly crossing FR 81 at the pass, climbs the edge of the lava
flow, then goes north and northwest to the Blue Lake trailhead. The
trail continues north, crossing Huckleberry Saddle then dropping to
the banks of the South Fork Toutle River, a total of 13.5 miles and six
trail junctions.

The trail section described here goes to Redrock Pass and is not
heavily used by hikers as the lure of the higher trails is a siren call. In
addition, the lower section to McBride Lake is used by horseback riders. From the trailhead the trail goes through a mixed forest of lodgepole and fir with the Kalama River often in sight. It is an attractive
trail if one wants total enclosure in forest. At 3.8 miles most equestri-
ans turn onto FR 600 and go north, cross FR 81, and continue onto
the Blue Lake Horse Trail that climbs through lodgepole forest to the
Blue Lake Mudflow and on to Huckleberry Saddle.

For those who want to sample this trail, hike the section from
Redrock Pass to the lake, then to FR 600, and perhaps west briefly onto
the level forest trail toward the trailhead. The McBride Lake section

Opposite: Waterfall on Sheep Canyon Creek near Toutle Trail 238

from FR 600 to the pass is 1.8 miles, not counting the 0.3 mile from FR 81 to the trail.

McBride Lake Section. At Redrock Pass the trail climbs the south side and in 250 yards enters a beautiful grove of old growth. The trail here is attractive and remains on a steep hillside with many small ups and downs. Just before reaching the lake you go through another grove of giant trees. Look down onto the lake and enjoy several good, screened views of St. Helens. The trail continues descending. At the lake's west end, leave the trail for a lakeside rest.

If you have children, an easier way to reach the lake is to walk in on FR 600, then 0.4 mile to the lake itself. There is no beach.

Mountain Biking. From Redrock Pass the tread is generally good with several abrupt ups and downs. Several side stream crossings are rough. It is mostly downhill, except for the initial short climb from the pass.

■ ■

21. Toutle Trail 238:
BLUE LAKE TO SOUTH FORK TOUTLE RIVER

A climb past Blue Lake into old growth, over Huckleberry Saddle, down to Sheep Creek

Length ■ Sheep Canyon 3 miles, South Fork Toutle Canyon 4.5 miles

Difficulty ■ Moderate

Users ■ Hikers, Mountain bikers, Horseback riders to Sheep Canyon bridge only

Elevation ■ Trailhead 3,213 feet, saddle 3,953 feet, Sheep Canyon 3,640 feet, South Fork Toutle 3,220 feet

Maps ■ (Maps 14, 15, 16), Green Trails 364, 364S (partial coverage), USGS Goat Mountain, Mount St. Helens

Season ■ Late June through September

Driving Directions ■ Drive to the junction of FR 81 and FR 8123, then north on FR 8123 for 1.5 miles to the Blue Lake trailhead.

Considering the full 13.5-mile length of the Toutle Trail, this section to the Toutle River is the most beautiful and varied.

Trailhead to Sheep Canyon. Hike north from the trailhead and soon pass above Blue Lake, which is not blue but a stunning emerald even on cloudy days. The small lake was formed 600 years ago by a mud-flow that blocked the creek, and the standing silver snags in the lake and the gravel beds attest to this event. Beyond the lake the trail climbs through old growth, then eases off at an old clearcut hillside. An un-usual meadow (a dry campsite) 500 yards before Huckleberry Saddle provides a good view of St. Helens. Reenter old growth and descend to a junction with the Sheep Canyon Trail. Here at a complex meeting of trails are two bridges. The upper bridge leads up the Sheep Canyon Trail to the Loowit, and the lower goes to the Toutle River. If you cross neither, in 0.7 mile you will reach the Sheep Canyon trailhead at the end of FR 8123.

There is lovely trailside greenery, sorrel, hellebore, and thousands of avalanche lilies in early summer. The giant noble firs provide deep shade for the bunchberries, candyflower, and vanilla leaf plants. As you descend to the bridges there are views across the Toutle to high ridges, some with blasted forest and some previously clearcut.

As you arrive at the bridges you have three choices, all rewarding and described here: explore down to the Sheep Canyon trailhead, con-tinue to the Toutle River, or climb the Sheep Canyon Trail to the Loowit.

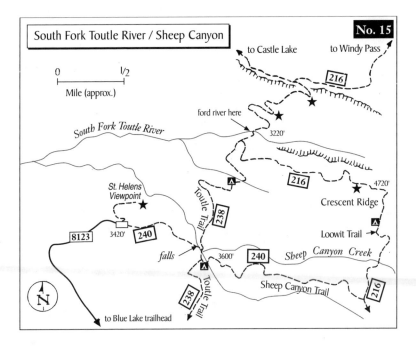

Sheep Canyon to South Fork Toutle River. This section of the trail that goes to the South Fork Toutle River junction with the Loowit Trail is similar to the first 0.7 mile of the Sheep Canyon Trail from its trailhead to the bridges: beautiful old growth on steep hillsides. As you hike toward the Toutle through lovely forest you will reach the edge of green forest and have views. Where the dead, standing forest merges with the green forest, look across to the high north wall above the Toutle, a steep area of green hillsides, and farther east a huge sandy hillside where the Loowit Trail climbs onto Castle Ridge 700 feet above the river. Here in the transition zone between scorched, dead trees and green forest look down onto a delta and long beaver dams very near an excellent creekside campsite. Beyond, several obvious, steep elk trails cross your trail and lead down to the Toutle. At the campsite look for the chaos of trees that crashed down in a huge landslide from the opposite steep hillside in February 1996.

The trail crosses the creek, then the slide area, and climbs around

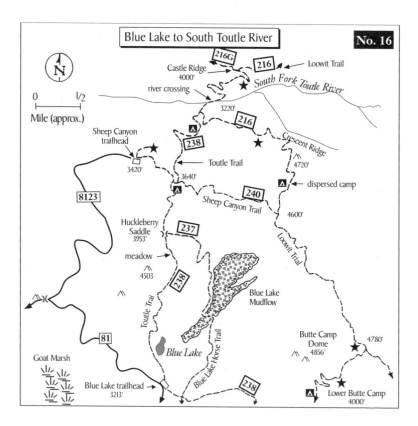

The high pumice slope on the Loowit Trail leading up to Castle Ridge above the South Fork Toutle River valley, with a trail work party of the Northwest Youth Corps

the ridge to sandy, desertlike slopes. Even here you will see penstemon, Indian paintbrush, and dwarf lupine. At the river's edge are great stands of alders, all naturally regenerated after the entire valley was scoured in 1980.

As you stand at the edge of the Toutle, you again have three choices: cross the river and climb the trail for incredible views back down the valley; return the way you came; or, with more effort, climb the Loowit up onto Crescent Ridge for views that stretch to the Coldwater Ridge Visitor Center and up to the mountain far above. The Crescent Ridge hike takes you to the Sheep Canyon Trail, your route back to the Toutle Trail (see trail description 27).

Mountain Biking. These trails all have good, solid treads for biking, but there are many steep sections and intimidating, very steep sidehills and dropoffs.

■ ■

22. Blue Lake Horse Trail 237

An alternative return loop on a mudflow with views of St. Helens

Length ■ Blue Lake Horse Trail 5.3 miles, Loop 5.6 miles
Difficulty ■ Moderate
Users ■ Hikers, Mountain bikers, Horses

Elevation ▪ Low Point 2,700 feet, Huckleberry Saddle 3,953 feet,
    Blue Lake Trailhead 3,213 feet
Maps ▪ (Maps 14, 16), USGS Goat Mountain, Mount St. Helens
Season ▪ Late June through September
Driving Directions ▪ Drive to the junction of FR 81 and FR 8123,
    then north on FR 8123 to Blue Lake trailhead.

The lower end of the horse trail starts at a junction with the Toutle
Trail just west of McBride Lake. It then goes north on FR 600, crosses
FR 81, plunges into lodgepole pine forest on a sandy, loose tread,
climbs 1,253 feet to Huckleberry Saddle on the Toutle Trail (crossing the Blue Lake Mudflow en route), and feeds into an old logging
road for the final distance to the saddle. In winter, the horse trail is
used by snowmobiles.

Constructed primarily for the use of horseback riders, and with
help from volunteer riders, the Blue Lake Horse Trail extends 5.3 miles
from south to north, ending at Huckleberry Saddle. However, the upper 3 miles of this trail can serve as the east leg of a loop starting at the
Blue Lake trailhead. The loop goes up the beautiful Toutle Trail to the
saddle, then back down its east leg: the upper Blue Lake Horse Trail.
The loop offers variety and views not found when hiking directly up
the Toutle Trail and back down, and in addition provides an adventuresome alternative. For those who want to hike the loop, see trail
descriptions 20 and 21. The following is a description of the loop's east
leg down from the saddle.

From the saddle hike east on a wide, sandy trail, which is actually
an old logging road. The trail circles to the east side of a large clearcut
that is now regrowing into thick alpine fir forest. Along the trail sides
are tall, old-growth noble firs. At 0.9 mile from the saddle leave the
road and climb east onto a trail that is obscure and poorly marked. Enter
forest and wind 0.3 mile through meadows and lodgepole forest, coming out onto the edge of the large mudflow. Enjoy the view of St.
Helens, then continue south, downhill, and enter attractive forest west
of the mudflow.

Follow as well as possible the poorly defined trail and cross the
rocky mudflow. Pass near an unusual, solitary tall fir tree in the middle
of the mudflow. Enter the forest on the east side, and 2.1 miles from
where you left the old logging road come to a four-way trail junction.
To the southeast 3.2 miles is Redrock Pass. At the junction, the Blue
Lake Horse Trail continues south 2 miles to FR 81. To complete the
loop, turn right at the four-way and hike 0.3 mile west to the Blue Lake
trailhead.

Mountain Biking. From the Blue Lake trailhead and north on the Toutle Trail, the tread is firm but steep to Huckleberry Saddle. The remainder of the loop is generally unsuitable for bikes as the trails are soft and sandy, and bikes must be carried across the wide mudflow.

23. Loowit Trail 216:
ROUND-THE-MOUNTAIN

An extraordinarily scenic trail
with sweeping vistas through a wide variety of terrains

Length ▪ Approximately 30 miles, depending on access trail
Difficulty ▪ Very difficult
Users ▪ Backpackers, Hikers, Mountain bikers on some segments
Elevation ▪ Loowit low point 3,220 at South Fork Toutle River; high point 4,885 feet at Windy Pass; lowest feeder trail 2,700 feet

Upper canyon of South Fork Toutle River from Loowit Trail on Crescent Ridge with Castle Ridge at center, Johnston Ridge in distant right, Elk Rock in distant center

Cumulative Gain ■ 5,000 feet plus
Maps ■ (Maps 11, 17, 18), Green Trails 364, 364S, USGS Mount
    St. Helens
Season ■ Late June through September
Driving Directions ■ See the trail description for details.

The Loowit Trail circling Mount St. Helens is a world-class scenic
adventure and one of the most interesting and challenging trails of the
Northwest. Like the Wonderland Trail of Mount Rainier (90 miles)

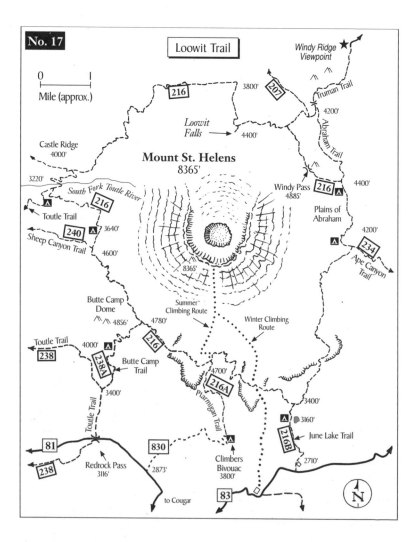

and the Timberline Trail of Mount Hood (38 miles), most of the trail is at or above timberline. Unlike these two famous trails, all of the Loowit's miles were affected by recent volcanic activity.

It is important to know that the full trail, indeed even sections of it, is exhausting and difficult. The loop is for experienced travelers who are in good physical condition and are confident and experienced with difficult conditions. Although most backpackers plan on three days, many who have done so advise four days. You are contending not just with miles but also with countless ups and downs, innumerable gullies, dry washes, and canyons of every size, often with poor footing on steep, unstable slopes that intimidate even the most experienced.

Visitors coming from Portland/Vancouver begin a 3-day hike of this 30-mile route at either the Ptarmigan Trail or June Lake. To take best advantage of elevation gain and loss for maximum miles per day, the best hiking direction is counterclockwise, leaving the longest section for the last day. Camping sites are limited, and hiking days are determined by campsites to protect the fragile environment of soft pumice, ash, and struggling plant life. Most hikers camp on the Plains of Abraham, in the South Fork Toutle River area, and in the June Lake area. The 10-mile section of the northside Restricted Area is closed to all off-trail travel and camping.

If you are coming from Seattle drive to St. Helens's south side to start the 3-day trip. Some visitors start from Windy Ridge ending their first day at the South Fork Toutle and making second camp at June Lake.

There are eight feeder trails to the Loowit that give access for splendid 1-day loops or out-and-back explorations. If a car shuttle is not used to complete a loop, a bicycle can be left for the closing of a loop's final leg on either FR 81 or FR 83. The Castle Ridge feeder is not a practical access as it is reached only by remote, private Weyerhaeuser Company roads. The Loowit is not crossed by a single road, and the shortest and lowest access is the June Lake Trail.

The Loowit is remarkable in its variety of terrain. There are only three short sections of old growth to enjoy; the remainder is dry and shadeless. Lava flows are crossed in four places, and there are innumerable dry gullies. Both small and large, deep canyons often present problems with footing and balance on the loose ash and rock sidewalls. A walking staff or ski poles provide not only balance but a measure of safety, particularly when carrying a heavy pack. The trail is marked in featureless areas such as the Pumice Plain and lava flows with tall posts, surveyor stakes, and rock cairns.

You will note extraordinary contrasts as you cross the northside

Restricted Area: smooth pumice plains; wrinkled areas with countless small washout drainages; springs that cannot be counted on for drinking water all summer; wide, deep gullies and deep canyons and boulder and lava ridges; amazing oases of greenery; and above all sweeping views. Do not count on finding water where maps show stream lines.

The loop should not be hiked in bad weather as there is virtually no shelter along the trail. In times of poor visibility, the trails crossing the lava flows, pumice plains, and rocky areas of the east and north sides would be impossible to follow in many places.

Detailed descriptions of the seven sections of the Loowit Trail follow.

Mountain Biking. This entire loop is open to bikers, except the Restricted Area on the mountain's north side from the Abraham/Loowit Trails junction (north end of the Plains of Abraham) to Castle Ridge above the South Fork Toutle River, a distance of 9.8 miles. Several sections of the remaining loop, however, are not recommended. The following descriptions provide more information.

Rock cairn and trail posts on the Plains of Abraham, with Windy Pass on the right

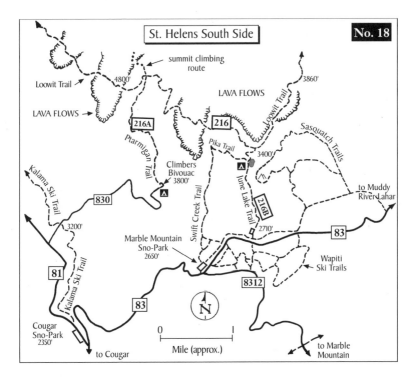

24. Loowit Trail 216:
PLAINS OF ABRAHAM TO CASTLE RIDGE
Very demanding and scenic trail across pumice deserts,
innumerable gullies, canyons, rocky terrain

Length ▪ Ape Canyon Trail to Castle Ridge 12.6 miles
Difficulty ▪ Very difficult
Users ▪ Hikers, Backpackers
Elevation ▪ Low point 3,680 feet, high point Windy Pass 4,885 feet
Cumulative Gain ▪ Approximately 2,000 feet
Maps ▪ (Maps 11, 17, 19), Green Trails 364, 364S, USGS Mount
   St. Helens

Season ■ Late June to September
Driving Directions ■ See directions for Ape Canyon Trail (trail description 35) and Plains of Abraham (trail description 10).

This section of the Loowit Trail is the most physically demanding due to the rough terrain and the distance. Loop hikers frequently camp near Pumice Butte at the south end of the Plains as there is often water there; at the western end, they camp at the South Fork Toutle River.

From the junction of Ape Canyon Trail and Loowit Trail ascend the trail up a wide, rocky, shallow basin onto the Plains. Cross the nearly level, smooth pumice plain where rock cairns mark the route. At the junction with the Abraham Trail turn left and head for Windy Pass crossing several dry washes. Water may be found coming from an unusual, small lupine-covered basin. Reach the foot of Windy Peak and gain the trail as it climbs steeply on loose pumice, zigzagging twice. It is a grind to reach the pass where a strong wind and grand views of the Pumice Plain, Johnston Ridge, the backcountry peaks, and Rainier will greet you.

Chipped and blasted out of the rocky hillside, the trail descends steeply, making several switchbacks. It soon crosses a gully onto the Pumice Plain. Follow black cairns across a desolate landscape, with an occasional rare alder or fireweed, to the Windy Trail junction. The next 1.3 miles cross chaotic terrain with many gullies and a remarkable green oasis with water, to reach the Loowit Falls side trail. A precarious viewpoint at the edge of a vertical cliff appears after a 400-yard climb of about 200 feet. The 250-foot falls drop into a dark, narrow canyon.

Back at the Loowit Trail, turn left and walk 150 yards west to the crater-warmed creek. Cross and walk downhill 100 yards and recross the creek to its east side, where you descend the Sasquatch Steps 1 mile over rough rocks on an ill-defined trail marked by cairns down to the edge of the Pumice Plain. Turn and hike west crossing many draws and gullies. The trail climbs to cross a broad saddle at 4,040 feet on Studebaker Ridge, then the route turns southward on a very difficult section with many steep, nasty ravines and small canyons, many up to 40 or more feet deep.

The trail eventually reaches wide green slopes near the edge of the South Fork Toutle canyon. Hike down along the edge with fine views through blow-down into the wild, deep gorge. The ridge edge that

Opposite: On the Loowit Trail crossing the pumice desert of the Plains of Abraham, St. Helens sweeping upward from the Plains (Ann Marshall)

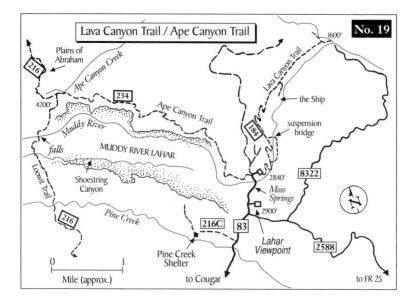

continues northwest from where the Loowit drops into the canyon is out of the Restricted Area, so camping is permitted, but the area has no water.

The South Fork Toutle River is another 0.9 mile down, in addition to the 12.6 from the Plains of Abraham.

25. Loowit Trail 216:
SOUTH FORK TOUTLE RIVER TO CASTLE RIDGE
From South Fork Toutle terraces to a ridge top with spectacular views

Length ▪ 0.9 mile
Difficulty ▪ Moderate
Users ▪ Hikers
Elevation ▪ Low point 3,280 feet, high point 4,000 feet
Maps ▪ (Maps 15, 16), Green Trails 364, 364S, USGS Mount St. Helens

Loowit Trail on the west side of St. Helens and upper Sheep Creek Basin, where a primitive campsite is located

Season ▪ Late June through September
Driving Directions ▪ See directions for Sheep Canyon Trail (trail
   description 27).

See trail description 21 (Toutle Trail) for the trail from Sheep Canyon to the Toutle River.

Then cross the South Fork Toutle River on stones (no bridge) and
watch for markers. Scramble up unstable debris onto a low terrace to
where the trail is well defined. The trail on both sides of the river, descending into and out of the river bottom, is poorly defined and subject to erosion and changes. Maintaining a rock-cleared trail and bridge
is impossible due to fluctuating river levels and floods.

The river crossing usually presents no problems; just find the right
combination of rocks. If you are carrying a heavy pack, try your selected crossing first without your pack to gain confidence and to verify
stability of the rocks. The water may be so high that rock hopping is
impossible. If so, remove your socks and wade in camp shoes or boots.
Wading in bare feet or socks alone may result in foot injuries. This
river, fed by high snowfields and remnant glaciers, is typical of mountain streams—as the day warms, the water volume increases and an
afternoon crossing may be more difficult. The Toutle, while not a large
river by any means, is the largest on the mountain proper.

After you have crossed the Toutle and are heading upward on Castle
Ridge, the first leg of the trail is fairly level, passing through an old
clearcut. Switchback and climb moderately through small alders and
maples to the next switchback at the very edge of the Toutle River, now
a canyon. Here, 0.5 mile along the trail, the view is stupendous, and if
you climb another 400 yards to the next switchback viewpoint you will
be rewarded even more. From either of the viewpoints the view sweeps
down miles of the wide, flat-bottomed Toutle valley bordered by green
hills. Directly below are greatly eroded debris terraces covered with
an unusual yellow moss, a striking contrast to the gray, rocky canyon.
Below, the Toutle is one stream formed by the confluence of two steeply
descending mountain streams, each in its own deep canyon. One canyon parallels Crescent Ridge (Loowit Trail route) and the other drops
steeply down directly from the mountain itself.

The scene is gigantic, and for one who has never trekked the mountains of Asia, it may appear to be Himalayan—stark, raw, rocky, and
wild. From the higher viewpoint it is only 300 yards to the Loowit Trail
junction with Castle Ridge Trail 216G (recently unmarked, overgrown,
and not visible). If you turn and walk down the ridge northwestward from the junction, you will enter an eerie forest of downed

and half-buried trees jutting skyward at a 30-degree angle. From the junction, the Loowit climbs quickly to the edge of a rolling, green plateau. The sandy terrain is sparsely covered with grasses and countless downed tree trunks, bleached and all pointing northwestward. Purple lupine is profusely scattered over large areas, with some Indian paintbrush and a few orange tiger lilies.

Of course, the mountain's presence is overpowering, rising far overhead. Views to the north include both the Coldwater Ridge and Johnston Ridge Visitor Centers and the peaks of the Mount Margaret Backcountry with Rainier behind. This is a spectacular site for a dry camp as it is just outside the Restricted Area.

■ ■

26. Loowit Trail 216:
SOUTH FORK TOUTLE RIVER
TO SHEEP CANYON

*From the deep Toutle canyon to a high ridge
with meadows and sweeping views*

Length ■ One way 2.7 miles, loop 7 miles
Difficulty ■ Moderate
Users ■ Hikers, Mountain bikers
Elevation ■ Toutle River 3,220 feet, high point 4,720 feet
Maps ■ (Maps 15, 16), Green Trails 364, 364S, USGS Goat Mountain, Mount St. Helens
Season ■ July through September
Driving Directions ■ See directions for Sheep Canyon Trail 240 (trail description 27).

From the junction of the Toutle and Loowit Trails, climb open, desolate slopes, then hike through thick thimbleberry bushes onto a forested ridge. As you climb the steep trail the views become increasingly impressive and soon you are level with the blow-down plateau across the canyon where the Loowit Trail tops the high, sandy slope. Soon you will see Coldwater Ridge Visitor Center and the Johnston Ridge

Junction of Loowit and Butte Camp Trails on southwest side of Mount St. Helens

Observatory building 5 miles away and then the entire Mount Margaret Backcountry range with its several high peaks spread out in front of Mount Rainier.

As you reach the green meadows the trail eases off to a comfortable angle. To the east is a deep, dusty canyon: headwaters for the Toutle. Dead, blasted, and uprooted trees with complex root systems in the air lie in profusion on this ridge. In spite of the deep covering of ash and pyroclastic flow debris that fell here, there has been a remarkable recovery with dense areas of huckleberry bushes, bear grass, sedges, and grasses crowding the trail.

Higher up, pass areas with bleached and broken standing trees next to green forest, then enter a beautiful, young forest of alpine fir with a meadowlike carpet of grasses. These trees, some up to 20 feet in height, were protected by deep snow and survived the May 18, 1980 blast that killed the larger trees.

Turn with the trail as it descends southward along sandy, gray slopes covered with great numbers of purple penstemon flowers and brilliant orange Indian paintbrush. The trail circles a wide gray basin with several ravines joining to form the head of Sheep Canyon. Just below the trail are several small ponds in a green area that is one of the few good campsites along this trail. This is a dramatic setting with the mountain rising above wide, green slopes.

Cross several trail washouts and climb out of the far side of the basin, walk through forest and into and out of shallow draws to the top of the Sheep Canyon Trail. To complete a loop, hike down the Sheep Canyon Trail.

Mountain Biking. This section of the Loowit is open to bike use but is very steep and has many areas of soft ash and pumice.

■■■■■■■■■■■■■■■■■■■■■■■■■■■■■■■■■■■■■ ■

27. Sheep Canyon Trail 240:
CRESCENT RIDGE

*Very scenic high country with views of St. Helens,
Johnston Ridge, canyons, and the blast zone*

Length ■ FR 8123 trailhead to Toutle Trail 0.7 mile, Toutle Trail to Loowit Trail 1.6 miles
Difficulty ■ Moderate
Users ■ Hikers, Mountain bikers
Elevation ■ Trailhead 3,420 feet, Loowit Trail 4,600 feet
Maps ■ (Maps 15, 16), Green Trails 364, 364S, USGS Goat Mountain, Mount St. Helens
Season ■ Late June through September
Driving Directions ■ From the junction of FR 81 and FR 8123, drive 8123 6.6 miles to its end.

Before starting on the trail consider the 400-yard Viewpoint Trail from the parking area, an easy out-and-back walk to views of the South Fork Toutle River valley and the edge of the lateral blast zone of 1980. Descend through an old clearcut, now a jungle of alder and maple, and walk to the trail's end through tall, bleached, branchless snags killed by the blast of super-heated gasses traveling at hundreds of miles per hour. Nearby are trees that survived, creating a condition of mixed dead and green forest you will also see on Crescent Ridge. Note in the distance the different directions that trees were blown down. The full view of St. Helens here is the last you will have for an hour or more until you are much higher on the trail.

Once on the trail climb gentle grades into refreshingly cool old growth and walk along a ledgelike trail clinging to the steep mountainside. Look straight out at the towering tree trunks. The trailside greenery of devils club, mosses, ferns, and other species makes for an enchanted forest experience.

As you near the complex trail junction with the Toutle Trail be sure to walk out to a nearby view of the canyon and waterfall. As you look up Sheep Canyon you can see how in 1980 the enormous quantity of flood debris roared down the steep confines of the mountainside chasm, scouring and stripping everything in its path, sloshing and ricocheting from side to side, uprooting trees on both sides and carrying them many miles down the Toutle River.

At the junction cross the upper bridge, pass a good campsite, and climb moderate grades through old growth. As you gain elevation note how the forest type changes to subalpine and silver fir, slender, spirelike, and draped with long witch's hair lichen growth. Climb through this increasingly picturesque area to the Loowit Trail at timberline.

For the best views, turn north on the Loowit and climb into green meadows at the edge of the blast zone where many silver snags still stand beside green forest, and many others lie in the green meadows blown downhill. From the high point there are sweeping views to the Coldwater Visitor Center and Johnston Ridge Observatory 5 miles

Loowit Trail crossing a lava flow between Butte Camp Trail and Ptarmigan Ridge. Mount Adams and Indian Heaven skyline are beyond.

away, as well as a panoramic view of the high peaks above Spirit Lake.

Mountain Biking. The trail up is a "pusher," but a great downhill run on a generally firm, obstacle-free tread. Higher up, a few rocks and water bars will slow you down.

■■■■■■■■■■■■■■■■■■■■■■■■■■■■■■■■■■■

28. Loowit Trail 216:
SHEEP CANYON TO BUTTE CAMP TRAIL
Very scenic, high-country travel across mostly above-timberline terrain

🚶🚶

Length ■ 2.8 miles
Difficulty ■ Easy, with one difficult canyon crossing
Users ■ Hikers
Elevation ■ High point 4,800 feet; low point 4,600 feet
Maps ■ (Maps 15, 16, 17), Green Trails 364, 364S, USGS Mount St. Helens
Season ■ Late June through September
Driving Directions ■ See directions to Toutle Trail (trail description 21) and those for Butte Camp Trail (trail description 29).

From Sheep Canyon travel south, rounding minor ridges through light forest, mostly lodgepole pine, silver fir, and some whitebark pine. Soon arrive at a deep, V-shaped canyon with the northside trail on a descending angle to the bottom. This slope is not unlike the side of a glacial moraine—loose rock and sand, and intimidating.

It is an impossible hundred feet or so to maintain so it will always be troublesome. If you are hiking from south to north, it may look impossible and vertical. Other hikers will have crossed before you so normally there will be steps kicked into the loose wall, often supported by loose-looking stones. Be very cautious, perhaps trying first without a pack if yours is heavy, to test the crossing both physically and mentally. A hiking staff or ski poles could be a great advantage here for balance and confidence. There may be snow in the canyon bottom, which is not a problem unless it is icy. The opposite wall (northfacing) is only a short, steep scramble up rubble.

Once across, the route southward passes through lovely stands of pines, but most of it crosses high meadows with rocky outcrops. Above, the mountain rises in great sweeps of green slopes, basins, and snow-fields.

The trail meanders delightfully from ridge to ridge, and between are shallow draws and open basins. There are many flowers in early summer—ground-hugging wild strawberry, dwarf lupine, penstemon, and occasional phlox cushions. Above the trail look for grassy draws with morainelike black lava walls.

Unusually large cushions of phlox flowers on the Loowit Trail east of Ptarmigan Ridge

Early on the trail, trees fight their way up ridges far above your route. It is a rugged scene, constantly changing and always surprising with new vistas. As you near Butte Camp Dome (two low, forested buttes), cross a pumice plain, actually an ancient debris flow. Continue across the debris flow to a series of low ridges skirting the wrinkled mountainside. This high, above-timberline area is exceedingly lovely with many flowers in early summer. At the junction with the Butte Camp Trail, enjoy the beauty of the open, grassy slopes and the picturesque low ridge traversed by that trail.

■ ■

29. Toutle Trail 238:
BUTTE CAMP TRAIL 238A

Most scenic access to the Loowit Trail
and above-timberline hiking with sweeping views

Length ■ To Loowit Trail 3.9 miles
Difficulty ■ Moderate
Users ■ Hikers
Elevation ■ Redrock Pass 3,116 feet, Lower Butte Camp 4,000 feet,
    Loowit Trail 4,800 feet
Maps ■ (Map 14), Green Trails 364, 364S, USGS Mount St. Helens
Season ■ Late June through September
Driving Directions ■ Drive to junction of FR 81 and FR 8123, then
    drive east on FR 81 2.5 miles to Redrock Pass, or drive west 2.8
    miles on FR 81 from the junction of FR 81 and 83.

At Redrock Pass climb the low edge of the lava flow for a fine view of St. Helens. Cross the lava flow on a paved path to meadows in a setting of alpine fir. Here you will see penstemon flowers, bushy heads of bear grass, wild strawberries, and lupine flowers. In 1.2 miles arrive at a junction with Trail 238A, the route to Lower Butte Camp, and to the forested volcanic "dome" near timberline. At this junction Trail 238 veers northwest for 3.4 miles. It passes through mixed forest, crosses a wide, rocky lahar, reenters forest, then crosses the Blue Lake Horse Trail before arriving at the Blue Lake trailhead.

On the Loowit Trail east of Ptarmigan Ridge looking across a lava flow to Mount Adams

From the junction hike up Trail 238A through open stands of lodgepole pine and western hemlock. The trail climbs moderately as it winds its way to Lower Butte Camp at 4,000 feet and 2.5 miles from the pass. The camp is a lovely level area of small meadows, subalpine fir, and a nearby creek. If water is not available here, hike up the trail 200 yards, then look for water to the left. The area has many flowers—phlox, hellebore, lupine, and yellow dandelion. It is a little paradise nestled at the base of steep slopes, except for the mosquitos.

Above the meadows, follow the trail as it climbs through wonderful old-growth noble fir and white fir. Notice the many trees with "snow knees," a curious bend in the lower trunk where the years of snow creep have affected the growth of the trunk.

Cross a dry hillside of pumice with many penstemon and lupine flowers, and at a turn enjoy a distant view of Hood and Jefferson. Follow the trail uphill through increasingly open areas until you reach the Loowit Trail, a gain of 1,590 feet from the pass. If you elect to hike more, go west along the near-level trail, crossing minor ridges and shallow basins with splendid views in all directions. If you hike east you will soon be on the rough surface of a large lava flow.

■ ■

30. Loowit Trail 216:
BUTTE CAMP TRAIL TO PTARMIGAN RIDGE
High-country timberline scenery and two big lava flows to cross

🚶🚶 🚲

Length ■ 2.5 miles
Difficulty ■ Moderate
Users ■ Hikers, Mountain bikers
Elevation ■ Loowit Trail low point 4,560 feet, high point 4,800 feet, Redrock Pass 3,116 feet
Maps ■ (Maps 14, 17), Green Trails 364, 364S, USGS Mount St. Helens
Season ■ July through September
Driving Directions ■ See directions for Butte Camp Trail 238A (trail description 29) and Ptarmigan Trail 216A (trail description 31).

This section of the Loowit is for day hikers wanting to experience travel on large lava flows. Hikers looking for a less demanding route can try the Loowit Trail section west of the Butte Camp Trail to Sheep Canyon (trail description 26).

From Butte Camp Trail hike east on the Loowit and soon climb and cross a 400-yard-wide black lava flow. Marked by tall posts and surveyor stakes, the trail is easy to follow if you stay alert. Although the lava surface is very rough, an excellent job was done making a reasonably easy tread to walk. At times, however, you will be hopping and stepping from one stone to another and working at maintaining your balance—especially if you are carrying a heavy, round-the-mountain pack or your bicycle.

Descend from the lava flow and cross a deep, steep-sided ravine with a small waterfall. The west wall of the ravine is unstable rock and ash, and the 100-foot diagonal descent calls for care. The ravine's other side is an easy, safe slope. With the lava flow behind, start crossing sandy and grassy hillsides and pass through alternating bands of pine and steep green slopes with sweet-smelling phlox cushions. Follow the wrinkled mountainside where subalpine fir and whitebark pine mix together. There are views to Hood and Jefferson. Look to the west for Goat Mountain with the bright green marsh at its base.

Now cross a much larger lava flow, some 800 yards across and 200 feet high, which descends far below you. Just beyond is a thick alpine fir forest with a minor ravine to cross. Recently the ravine was choked with trees carried down by snow avalanches passing through the basin at the head of the Ptarmigan Trail, where the climb of the mountain really begins. Look for these avalanche victims in the gully where they have been cut to provide trail passage. Just east of this avalanche gully is the Ptarmigan Trail and the end of this trail section.

Mountain Biking. Although officially designated for mountain biking, this trail is not well suited for bicycles due to two large, difficult lava flows and otherwise soft pumice trails.

■ ■

31. Ptarmigan Trail 216A

Access to Loowit Trail and Monitor Ridge
climbing route and summit through steep, thick forest

🚶🚶 🚲

Length ■ To Loowit 2.1 miles
Difficulty ■ Moderate
Users ■ Hikers, Climbers
Elevation ■ Trailhead 3,800 feet, Loowit Trail 4,700 feet
Maps ■ (Map 18), Green Trails 364, 364S, USGS Mount St. Helens
Season ■ Late June through September
Driving Directions ■ Drive to the junction of FR 83 and FR 81, drive
    FR 81 1.6 miles to FR 830, then uphill 2.5 miles on FR 830 to the
    Climbers' Bivouac, a large parking lot trailhead with limited dis-
    persed camping sites for Monitor Ridge climbers (FR 830 is a well-
    maintained two-lane gravel road. This road is not plowed in spring
    so when it opens for vehicle traffic depends on snow melt, but it is
    usually open by late June. If it's not driveable, climbers should park
    as far up FR 81 as possible. There are restrooms at the Bivouac.
    Water is not available.)

This trail has only one function: to get you to the Loowit Trail or the Monitor Ridge climbing route to the summit of St. Helens. The trail climbs steeply and relentlessly through thick forest with no views. If you want a view, hike 350 yards east on the Loowit to a large grassy

June Lake, a pond ringed by forest, cliffs, waterfall and lava flow on south side of Mount St. Helens

hillside for down-mountain views to canyons and lava flows and east 34 miles to Mount Adams. For other views hike 300 yards west on the Loowit onto a lava flow. Or follow the Ptarmigan Trail above the Loowit 300 yards for a view of Adams and to a small snow basin at the foot of Monitor Ridge; the basin is also the edge of a steep-sided lava flow and the summit route is there, marked by posts.

Climbing. See the description for the Monitor Ridge Summit Climb (trail description route 40) for details of the climbing route above the Ptarmigan Trail.

■ ■

32. Loowit Trail 216:
JUNE LAKE TO PTARMIGAN RIDGE

Wild alpine scenery, steep mountainsides, old growth, remains of a huge avalanche, streams and lava flows, a small lake and waterfall

🚶🚶 🚲

Length ■ One way 4.7 miles
Difficulty ■ Difficult east to west
Users ■ Hikers, Mountain bikers

View from Loowit Trail looking down to Muddy River Lahar, the Ape Canyon Trail forested ridge, and across to Mount Adams

Elevation ▪ Trailhead 2,710 feet, Ptarmigan Trail 4,700 feet, gain 2,000 feet

Maps ▪ (Maps 17, 18), Green Trails 364, 364S, USGS Mount St. Helens

Season ▪ Late June through September

Driving Directions ▪ See directions for Loowit Trail (trail description 33).

June Lake, a shallow pond in a scenic, cliff-bound basin with a waterfall, is popular with casual walkers and picnickers and is visited by serious hikers on their way to greater adventures on the Loowit Trail. There is a good campsite near the lake.

This very scenic but demanding section of the Loowit Trail is best hiked from east to west. This means the out-and-back route first climbs to Ptarmigan Ridge, then returns on the same route downhill to your starting place at the June Lake trailhead. This is an energy-consuming hike that is often underestimated. Allow lots of time for enjoying the marvelous scenery and crossing extensive lava flows. Carry two quarts of water per person, particularly in hot weather.

From the trailhead the wide, heavily used trail winds uphill through tall, regenerating second growth. The trail has no views until just before the lake: a fine view of the mountain and a lava flow that descends from far up the mountain, then down past the lake and farther down the valley.

The small lake is shallow with a sandy bottom and crystal clear. In early summer a 70-foot waterfall, fed by an underground source, dashes onto rocks beside the lake. Partly enclosed by steep forest and tree-draped cliffs, the lake has an inviting sandy beach on its west shore. A good campsite with privacy is found 100 yards northwest of the lake near the edge of the forest and the lava flow.

To reach the Loowit Trail from the lake go to the lake's northwest corner and enter thick greenery. Climb a very steep 450 yards on a zig-zag route through old growth to the junction. The trail is packed dirt and dangerous when wet.

To hike to Ptarmigan Ridge, turn left at the junction. Soon reach a 200-foot lava flow up which the trail climbs steeply on a rugged, rocky trail. As on most lava flows, the tread is barely noticeable as you balance from rock to rock following surveyor stakes and tall trail marker posts.

It is a long haul across the half-mile-plus of lava, then across a pumice area with small firs to Swift Creek and its 40-foot box-canyon waterfall, called Chocolate Falls. The water runs down to the brink in interesting, water-worn channels.

Hike the trail uphill alongside the creek, then enter big timber. Before plunging into the steep hillside old growth, look upmountain at the enormous lava flows, the spectacular canyons, and a green, forested island that looks impossibly far above, yet soon you'll be looking directly across to it.

Climb steeply through the ancient forest with only a few views of Adams and the lava flow. Below you, then along the trail as you get higher, note hundreds of bleached tree trunks carried down in a long-ago massive snow avalanche. Perhaps as many as a thousand or more trees lie scattered by the avalanche that swept thousands of feet downward, wiping out trees across huge areas. Finally, cross a large, grassy, mountainside meadow on an almost level trail westward into a 350-yard section of old forest and suddenly arrive at the Ptarmigan Trail at 4,700 feet.

Arriving at the Ptarmigan Trail is anticlimactic as there are no views. Hike up the Ptarmigan Trail 300 yards for a view of Adams, then a view of the steep lava flow where the climbing route goes. Note also the many small firs pushed over by a 1996 snow avalanche that reached far enough down the hillside to block the Loowit Trail.

Mountain Biking. Although this section of the Loowit Trail is open to bikes, it is not recommended. The trail is very steep, and your bike will have to be carried across the wide, rough lava flow. There is almost no gentle or moderate terrain along this trail. If you ride this trail, do so west to east.

■ ■

33. Loowit Trail 216:
JUNE LAKE TO APE CANYON

Spectacular travel through old growth and across rough, scenic lava lands

Length ■ Trailhead to Ape Canyon 6.4 miles
Difficulty ■ Moderate, then difficult in canyons
Users ■ Hikers, Mountain bikers
Elevation ■ Trailhead 2,710 feet, high point 4,500 feet
Cumulative Gain ■ One-way 2,300 feet, round-trip 2,800 feet
Maps ■ (Maps 17, 18, 19), Green Trails 364, 364S, USGS Mount
St. Helens
Season ■ Late June through September
Driving Directions ■ Drive to junction of FR 83 and FR 81, then
drive FR 83 3.8 miles to turnoff for June Lake trailhead

For information on the June Lake Trail and area and access to the
Loowit Trail, read trail description 32 (June Lake to Ptarmigan Ridge
section of the Loowit Trail).

Climb from June Lake to the Loowit junction, then turn right and
soon meet a lava flow with good tread. Note a magnificent mountain
hemlock tree below the trail. Short Creek, flowing out of the lava just
below the trail, feeds the June Lake waterfall and is a source of water for
trail hikers. Cross the lava into nearby lichen-draped forest, then hike
along the base of the lava flow on the forest trail, pass a pond, and soon
enter an old clearcut. Ahead is a high, volcanic formation called Worm
Flows Buttress, a goal for backcountry skiers. To the south is Marble
Mountain, a nearby forested shield volcano, and beyond is Hood.

The trail steepens as you start up the open face of the buttress,
and it is a long climb as the trail circles around its east side. High on
the buttress start enjoying a panorama—the lower half of the Muddy
River Lahar, the Shoestring Glacier notch on the mountain's skyline,
Pine Creek Canyon, and Adams looming large. This is one of the finest views along the entire Loowit Trail.

Leave the buttress and wind through a picturesque, rocky area, then
to the upper reaches of Pine Creek, a barren, devastated gravel plain.
A trailside stump shows the height of the 1980 mudflow that roared

On the Ape Canyon Trail a 100-foot-deep slot in the rock wall where lahars of 1980 flowed over the cliff tops, stripping off trees

down the 80-foot-deep canyon, overflowing its high rim to grind down the stump.

Make the short, steep descent into, then out of, the Pine Creek gully on unstable surfaces and continue north into grassy meadows with sedges, bear grass, and huckleberry bushes in a ghost forest. Sweeping views of the volcanoes and St. Helens's lower slopes seem to get even better, and Rainier shows for the first time.

Enter a desertlike area of gravelly canyons and deep gullies, all from Shoestring Canyon above. There are two deep canyons, then two shallower ones to cross on what are often deteriorated trails on unstable, steep slopes.

A fifth, final deep canyon requires crossing. Then descend pumice slopes past a view of the canyon's 70-foot waterfall. For a description of this last 0.7 mile of trail, the trail description 35 (Ape Canyon Trail).

Mountain Biking. This is a difficult ride on a soft pumice trail with five steep canyons that require carrying your bike on unstable, steep slopes.

34. Lava Canyon Trail 184

Raging river in a deep gorge, unusual formations, waterfalls

🚶🚶 ♿

Length ▪ Main trail 2.9 miles, with suspension bridge loop and Ship
    Trail total 3.6 miles, barrier-free trail 0.4 mile
Difficulty ▪ Easy to suspension bridge, Difficult for remainder
Users ▪ Hikers, Wheelchair users
Elevation ▪ Trailhead 2,840 feet, lower end of trail 1,660 feet, el-
    evation loss/gain 1,180 feet, to suspension bridge 300-foot loss
Maps ▪ (Map 20), Green Trails 364, USGS Smith Creek Butte
Season ▪ Late June through September
Driving Directions ▪ Drive FR 83 to the junction of FR 83 and FR
    81, then drive FR 83 8.6 miles to the trailhead at the road's end.

The Lava Canyon Trail may be the most interesting trail of the entire monument—no sweeping vistas here, but the remarkable lava

Ancient ash and pyroclastic layers along the lower Ape Canyon Trail and
Muddy River Lahar where trees were stripped of bark in 1980

Suspension bridge on Lava Canyon Trail leading to loop return to trailhead

formations, the wild gorges, and many waterfalls all combine to display the power of nature. There is no better word than awesome to describe this trail. To fully appreciate the wild scene of lava formations, cliffs, vertical-walled gorges, and mountain torrents you must hike below the paved and planked barrier-free trail, but this is not to say this trail is devoid of exciting views. The Forest Service deserves credit for it and for the lower trail over difficult and steep terrain, which serves as an almost daring hiking trail through this unique canyon.

From the trailhead, where there are restrooms and picnic tables, walk down the wide, paved barrier-free trail as it turns and switchbacks along the canyon's side, past one viewing platform and ending at a second viewing site. Along this first 700 yards you will pass through ancient forest and see unusual lava formations, some smoothed and shaped by thousands of years of water passage, floods, and many mudflows from ancient eruptions. There is also a view of a splendid waterfall crashing into a pool surrounded by polished cliffs. For wheelchair users, the grade is a bit steep but manageable. Interpretive signs explain features of the canyon and how it was formed.

Boardwalk barrier-free trail on the Lava Canyon Trail

A 0.5-mile loop, starting at the lower end of the paved trail, requires off-trail walking on slabby lava, then along an uneven but easy route, down and up metal stairs, then across the 100-foot, narrow, bouncing suspension bridge at the lower end of the loop. Walking this loop clockwise or counterclockwise is equally rewarding.

A lava gorge descends through the middle of the loop where the Muddy River dashes and churns between vertical walls, careens in polished rock bowls, then finds itself crashing over several waterfalls. In the twisting gorge you will see columnar basalt and unusual islands of black lava that remained as surrounding, softer materials eroded away from the original, massive lava flow that filled the canyon.

A memorable feature of the canyon and gorges are the near-vertical chutes in the smooth, black basalt, which direct the pounding waters downward into pools and a twisting riverbed. The thundering water, particularly wild in early summer, and the numerous waterfalls—occasionally several in view at one time—create an unforgettable experience. When you continue your hike down the valley from the suspension bridge you are starting on an adventure. The trail narrows to barely wide enough for one hiker, then steepens as it works its way down and along the rocky face of the canyon. The rubble-strewn trail and the dropoffs to your right without restraining rails demand your full attention. At times you will find yourself unconsciously hugging the wall for security from the exposure to the long drops to the river far below.

From the suspension bridge descend 0.6 mile of steep, switch-backing, downhill trail to a 32-foot ladder at a vertical cliff. The February 1996 storm brought trees and rocks down a side gully here and almost carried away the ladder. Below the ladder is an idyllic stretch of trail with ferns, a small grove of alders, and a stream. Then you reach the marked side trail to the Ship, a high lava island in the canyon with tall trees growing on its summit. A steep trail climbs to its top passing through a garden paradise. On top, walk to the up-valley end and enjoy the view of the canyon. This is a good place to sit and have lunch.

Below the Ship Trail the main trail moderates as you descend the valley. Pass through a small meadow where lupine grows profusely in early season. Continue 300 yards to a young alder grove 50 feet above the river, but notice logs and a frayed stump attesting to the height of the 1980 mudflow. Just before this grove is a trailside old-growth tree with bark torn off by the mudflow to a height of 10 feet.

Continue down the trail through a jungle of growth. Then step out of the forest onto the upper end of a huge alluvial plain where young trees are struggling to grow on the pumice desert. The plain descends gently 3,000 feet to an old logging road and Smith Creek, which here joins the Muddy River just below the former hiker and horse bridge that suffered irreparable damage in 1996. The logging road goes north on a sandy route past washouts and up Smith Creek where a challenging trail goes 9 miles to Windy Ridge. The alluvial plain is covered with thick, spreading mats of manzanita and kinnikinnick, dwarf lupine, and large areas of moss. Erratic boulders sit scattered about, carried by the mudflow, and small trees are spread over the area.

If you suffer from fear of heights or have children with you, do not hike below the suspension bridge. The steep, uneven trail has dizzying drops into the gorge and requires your total attention, plus it will be slippery when wet.

This canyon and its narrow gorges are the result of thousands of years of water erosion and the grinding, abrasive power of mudflows. The catastrophic 1980 eruption, the melting glaciers, great snowfields, and millions of tons of rock and debris filled the canyon in a terrifying torrent of destruction. Thousands of trees were carried some 16 miles down to the Lewis River and then into the Swift Reservoir. Then, in a smaller way, the floods of February 1996 carried trees and debris from side gullies into the canyon and damaged the trail.

■ ■

35. Ape Canyon Trail 234

Climb through old growth to ridge-top views, then across a pumice desert

🚶🚶 🚲

Length ■ To Loowit Trail 5.5 miles
Difficulty ■ Moderate
Users ■ Hikers, Mountain bikers
Elevation ■ Trailhead 2,840 feet, Loowit Trail 4,200 feet, elevation gain 1,350 feet
Maps ■ (Map 10), Green Trails 364, 364S, USGS Mount St. Helens, Smith Creek Butte
Season ■ Late June through September
Driving Directions ■ Drive FR 83 to the intersection with FR 81, then drive FR 83 a further 8.4 miles to the trailhead 0.2 mile before the Lava Canyon trailhead and the end of FR 83.

As you start up the trail notice from the edge of the lahar the 20-foot-high banks of yellowish sand layers. These are deposits of pyroclastic flow debris interspersed with layers of mudflow from previous eruptions. Notice the scarred trunks of large trees with bark torn off by the 1980 mudflow. As you progress along the generally level trail for more than a mile, wandering in and out of small draws filled with flowers and greenery, notice how the mudflow climbed more than a hundred feet up the hillside to scour off all growth, now rapidly regenerating. At a point of land that was scoured enjoy the view of St. Helens above the mile-wide lahar. It is not easy to visualize that in 1980 the raging mudflow was up to 30 feet deep.

In a mile from the viewpoint enter old growth and climb steadily for 2 miles without a view. Reach the top of the ridge, now narrow, and start a descent past views of the lahar and of St. Helens, then past scorched trees, still standing.

Finally, off the ridge with a brief view of Rainier 43 miles away, enter a pumice desert area on the trail that follows the edge of a precipitous dropoff into Ape Canyon. Here an unusual wall of lava, with a 100-foot narrow vertical slot through which you can see far down into Ape Canyon miles below, blocked the enormous mudflows of May 18,

Opposite: Ladder on the lower Lava Canyon Trail

1980. See where the abrasive mudflow rode over the wall, scouring soil and trees from its top, then flowed down the canyon scouring miles of streamside trees.

Quickly reach the junction with the Loowit Trail with the mountain's east face soaring above. This is a spectacular site and an area that deserves further exploration with a choice of two short side trips from the junction.

Your most interesting choice is to go south. If you choose this route, you will climb across a pumice hillside covered with ground-hugging manzanita shrubs and gentian flowers amid the alpine firs. Round a shoulder and 400 yards from the Loowit Trail junction descend onto a pumice plain with many scattered, black boulders—a contrasting scene, with one red rock in the center. As beautiful as this is, however, do not linger long, and continue upward another 400 yards, cross a small ravine, then 300 dry, desolate yards to your final goal. Here at the edge of a canyon lies a 70-foot waterfall of snowmelt roaring off a cliff into a giant hole in a large snowbank deep in the spectacular, dark canyon. The snow is, no doubt, from springtime snow avalanches. It is a wild scene with nothing but rock, steep canyon walls, morainelike ridges, and the mountain far above. For more details of this section of the trail, see trail description 33 (June Lake to Ape Canyon).

Your other choice is to go north to the Plains of Abraham. This climb offers a totally different experience. From the junction wind your way upward across wastelands of pumice and rock, climbing a wide draw to the Plains, a nearly level coffee-colored desert of pumice. Here, the Plains rise smoothly to the foot of the mountain. Opposite are barren hills on the east side of the Plains, with dead trees angled across the crests.

The Plains were once a green paradise of meadows, flowers, and streams. On May 18, 1980 terrible mudflows destroyed and leveled the area, followed by numerous pyroclastic flows that deposited layers of pumice, ash, and debris.

The Loowit Trail goes north across the Plains to the Abraham Trail that crosses flowered ridges then drops to join the Truman Trail near Windy Ridge. Partway across the Loowit turns and climbs to Windy Saddle, then crosses the saddle and drops steeply onto the Pumice Plain of the north side.

Mountain Biking. The Ape Canyon Trail may be a "pusher" for some bikers, but it is a great descent with a generally smooth tread and few obstacles. The Plains of Abraham are open to bikers, and the bicycle route continues north on the Abraham Trail, which descends steep grades and two sand ladders to the Truman-Abraham Saddle. The

Viewing waterfalls from the top of the Ship lava formation, a side trail from the Lava Canyon Trail

Truman Trail to Windy Ridge is open to bicycles, but the Pumice Plain and the Loowit Trail to Windy Pass are not. See trail description 10 for more information.

36. Smith Creek Trail 225

A remote, U-shaped glacial valley, big scenery,
and little-used adventuresome trail

Length ▪ 9 miles one way
Difficulty ▪ Difficult
Users ▪ Hikers
Elevation ▪ Upper trailhead 4,320 feet, lower trailhead 1,660 feet, elevation gain (loss) 2,660 feet

Maps ▪ (Map 20), Green Trails 364, USGS Smith Creek Butte
Season ▪ Late June through September
Driving Directions ▪ To reach the southern trailhead, drive on FR
    83 to the junction with FR 81, then continue on FR 83 8.6 miles
    to the Lava Canyon trailhead.

Hiking down the Lava Canyon Trail may be the best access to the trail
as the bridge across the Muddy River at the end of FR 8322, the previous trailhead, was washed out in February 1996. If the flood damage
to FR 8322 is repaired, then it serves as a good access, but the Muddy
River will have to be forded, and in early summer that may be unsafe
due to large volumes of snowmelt. Another access is available, a 4-mile
road that descends to the Smith Creek trailhead through second growth
just north of Lava Canyon, leaving FR 83 between the Ape Canyon
and Lava Canyon trailheads. It is possible that an official access to the
trailhead for hikers has still not been established. Call the monument
for trailhead information.

    This little-used and overlooked trail offers great rewards for adven-
turers. From the Windy Ridge trailhead the trail plunges more than
2,000 feet in the first 4.3 miles down an open ridge to the creek bottom. From the lower trailhead, the trail ascends the deep, impressive
valley on a route that likely involves some routefinding on unmarked
trail.

    There are two directions in which to hike the trail: from the top
end and then downhill, the preferred route, or from the bottom and

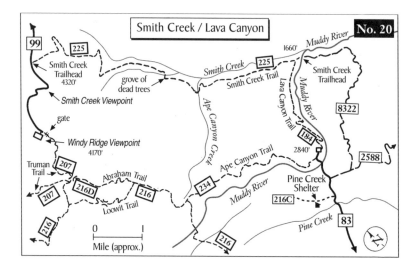

Washed out hikers' bridge across Muddy River near bottom of Lava Canyon. View is up Smith Creek to Windy Ridge

then uphill all the way. Either way requires an inconvenient car shuttle, unless the plan is to double back and retrace the outbound route. A car shuttle would involve FR 2588, a rough, 8-mile road, and FR 25.

From the North End Trailhead. From FR 99 the trail follows an abandoned, level logging road 0.4 mile, then drops around a ridge end and rock tower onto a hiking trail tread. Descend to a switchback (serious washout in 1996) and turn back to the wide ridge crest below the rock tower. Descend the wide ridge crest on soft pumice with blown-down trees and old logged stumps. Descend endlessly as the trail drops to a lower spur and goes westward, then cuts back and forth and finds the creek bottom. Here, it goes onto an irregularly shaped peninsula over 3 miles long with a creek on either side.

Hike along its flat surface through scattered trees to near its lower end. Reach a point opposite a unique grove of tall, standing, scorched trees on the creek's west bank. Climb down the bank, ford the creek, climb to the trail, and hike down the west bank to where Ape Canyon Creek crosses the trail. En route, pass through an amazing area of giant, blown-down trees, some half buried and angled up far into the air. Along the creek's terraced edge see extraordinary piles of driftwood. This 0.5-mile-long area of destruction is as impressive as the best examples anywhere in the monument.

At Ape Canyon Creek work your way across the flats through the vast collection of downed trees. Locate the trail opposite, climb through an old clearcut, join an abandoned road, and descend through a shady, leafy tunnel 0.4 mile. From here for the next 2 miles the trail

Smith Creek valley with Windy Ridge beyond. Logs litter the valley carried here by floods in 1980 and 1996

is impossible to describe coherently. You will be on the river flats part of the time, then climbing banks to get back on the road, washed out in many places, or onto segments of an unmarked foot trail, then the cycle of on, off, down, up repeats. Somehow it all works out, and with reasonable alertness you should find the hikeable road and trail sections with only a little frustration. Along the way enjoy good views of the wide, log-covered flats, and in one place walk through 500 yards of a magical tunnel of foliage over a section of old road.

You will eventually reach the wide alluvial fan of the Muddy River, across which the last 0.7 mile of the Smith Creek Trail passes.

From the South End Trailhead. The most scenic access to the Smith Creek Trail is to hike down the Lava Canyon Trail, which is more rewarding than the unmarked 4-mile road mentioned earlier. When FR 8322 is repaired, it will be the shortest access but will require fording the Muddy River.

From the bottom of the Lava Canyon Trail turn left at the bottom of the alluvial fan and follow a sandy, wide, level road north almost 0.7 mile to major road washouts. Work your way left around this, then read the previous description for a general idea of the route. The trail will eventually be marked, but even if not marked it is an interesting and worthwhile hike.

If you are on Windy Ridge and want to preview the trail, use your binoculars to examine the valley. From the base of the rock tower you can see all of it. The farthest open area is the Lava Canyon alluvial fan, and farther up is a grove of scorched, standing trees, landmark for the trail crossing to the long peninsula where the trail passes between two river flats. Identifying all this will make you feel comfortable about the challenge and exploratory aspects of your adventure.

■■■■■■■■■■■■■■■■■■■■■■■■■■■■■■■■■■■■■■■

37. Pine Creek Shelter and Lahar Trail 216C

Easy hike through towering fir to historic shelter and Muddy River Lahar

🚶 🚵

Length ■ Shelter 0.5 mile, lahar 0.8 mile
Difficulty ■ Easy
Users ■ Hikers, Mountain bikers
Elevation ■ Trailhead 2,980 feet, lahar 3,100 feet
Maps ■ (Maps 19, 20), Green Trails 364, USGS Smith Creek Butte
Season ■ Late June through September
Driving Directions ■ Drive FR 83 to the junction with FR 81, then drive FR 83 7 miles to the trailhead just east of the Pine Creek bridge

Enter the open-floored old growth on a wide, needle-covered path and climb almost imperceptibly for 500 yards to an old clearcut, now well reestablished with tall second growth. The trail, lined by lupine and scattered gentian, leads another 300 yards to a classic cedar shelter. This is a perfect hike with children and an ideal family picnic site.

The three-sided shelter was restored in 1991 and is used by cross-country skiers who have skied 4.5 miles up FR 83 from Marble Mountain Sno-Park. In the fall, it is home to hunters. There are two sleeping shelves and a small table and two chairs. Outside are two log benches. Rest for a moment on the outside benches, enjoy the quiet, and think of those who preceded you during the past 70 years. This trail was the original route to the Plains of Abraham (see trail description 35) until 1980 when much of the trail was destroyed by the gigantic mudflow down the Muddy River Lahar.

To explore the lahar and view Mount St. Helens, continue northeast past the shelter, about 600 yards down the trail. You will pass first through the regenerated clearcut, then through a fringe of old forest on the south edge of the mile-wide Muddy River Lahar.

Mountain Biking. It is a mostly solid tread to the shelter, and a lot of loose sand beyond.

■ ■

38. Muddy River Lahar and Vicinity

Remarkable view of St. Helens and eruption features

🚶🚶

Length ■ Short, casual walks
Difficulty ■ Easy
Users ■ Hikers
Elevation ■ General area about 2,900 feet
Maps ■ (Map 19), Green Trails 364, USGS Smith Creek Butte
Season ■ Late June through September
Driving Directions ■ Drive on FR 83 to the junction of FR 83 and FR 81, then drive FR 83 8 miles to the Lahar Viewpoint (Moss Springs and Stratigraphy Viewpoints are nearby).

There is only one word for the view of St. Helens from the Lahar Viewpoint in clear weather: magnificent! It sweeps across the mile-wide desert of the lahar and then climbs the east face of the mountain to its broken crest. It is particularly lovely in the soft light of early morning or with mid-afternoon shadows accenting features on the mountain's south side. In June and July the scene is further enhanced by wide areas of the lahar near the viewpoint covered by purple penstemon flowers.

For a better view from the Lahar Viewpoint, walk a few yards east onto the lower slopes of the forested hill. The enormous lahar, or mudflow as it is usually referred to, up to 30 feet deep and raging down the mountain in a devastating torrent, split here at this small hill, with one branch going down the Muddy River canyon (Lava Canyon Trail area) and the other going south down Pine Creek. A lone fir tree near the viewpoint shows its scar where the lahar scoured its bark at the height of the mudflow. At the viewpoint notice the fine gray dust at your feet. Take a pinch of the finest and blow it. This is the dense, heavy ash that traveled hundreds of miles. In Portland a thin layer on just a 50-by-100-foot lot totaled as much as 17 cubic feet, and a coating on the leaves of garden shrubs and trees remained stubbornly for months.

The Moss Springs Viewpoint is located 0.3 mile beyond the Lahar Viewpoint toward Lava Canyon. A 100-yard side road leads to a small parking area and short trail. Three large springs flow out of the lahar terminus and combine to form a sizeable stream, one of several to join the Muddy River, which then enters the Lava Canyon farther down. The Moss Springs are fed by rain, snow, and glacier melt that flows underground for more than 2 miles under the desertlike surface of the Muddy River Lahar.

Located 0.4 mile beyond the Lahar Viewpoint, the Stratigraphy Viewpoint sits at the edge of the Muddy River at the foot of the lahar. An interpretive panel describes the stream bank across the river where tephra deposits are interspersed with lahar deposits, and where at least seven layers are visible. The top layer is the deposit from the 1980 lahar. Note the living trees at the top of the stream bank with scarred trunks showing the maximum height of the 1980 mudflow.

39. Marble Mountain Sno-Park Trails

Easy to difficult ski trails traverse scenic meadows and climb to viewpoints

Length ▪ 5 trails, 0.5 mile to 10 miles round trip
Difficulty ▪ Mostly Easy or Moderate
Users ▪ Skiers
Elevation ▪ Sno-Park 2,650 feet
Maps ▪ (Map 18), Green Trails 3645
Season ▪ December through March
Driving Directions ▪ Drive FR 83 to the junction with FR 81, then another 3 miles on FR 83 to Marble Mountain Sno-Park.

From Marble Mountain Sno-Park there is a wide assortment of trails to choose among, most ranging from easy to moderate. If you are a backcountry skier and go beyond the trails you will be in some of the most spectacular skiing terrain in the Northwest. The following is a sampling of available trails and routes.

Wapiti Trails. These 5 miles of marked trails form several easy loops through Marble Mountain meadows and stands of alpine fir in a scenic setting nestled between the bases of both St. Helens and Marble Mountain, a neighboring shield volcano to the south. To ski the loops, cross snow-covered FR 83, the main snowmobile route, to the ski trails. The loops are named and well marked, and follow interesting and irregular courses with many gentle ups and downs. The Pine Marten Trail, across from and paralleling FR 83, has several access connectors to the Wapiti Trails.

Pine Marten Trail to June Lake. June Lake, a small pond nestled between forested cliffs and lava flow, is only 2.5 miles from the Sno-Park and therefore popular and often crowded. From the Sno-Park ski east 1.1 miles on the Pine Marten Trail, paralleling FR 83 but out of sight from the snowmobile traffic. This trail joins the 1.4-mile June Lake Trail. Both trails are rated as moderately difficult. Most of the distance is through forest and small meadows, with the last mile climbing to a viewpoint of St. Helens and the lava flow near the lake.

If you are looking for adventure, ski the Pika Trail, a 0.7-mile connector trail from the lake that climbs the lava flow northwestward and joins with the upper end of the Swift Creek Trail at 3,490 feet. The short trail is scenic and a worthy side trip from the lake. It is possible, however, to ski down the Swift Creek Trail to complete a 5.5-mile loop, although skiing up this trail is usually the best and easiest way to start the loop from the Sno-Park. The loop requires good downhill skiing skills.

Sasquatch Trails. The trails form two loops northeast of the Sno-Park totaling 7 miles, but you will have to ski the Pine Marten Trail 2.3 miles to reach them. Sasquatch Butte at 3,546 feet is the high point and is worth the final struggle up the last short slopes to its summit for the inspiring, panoramic views. Most of the area is rated moderate, and some downhill skills add to the enjoyment of the tour. The upper leg of the highest loop gives easy access through a thin band of forest to the Worm Flows Buttress (elevation 4,300 feet), a steep-faced lava flow with a flat summit and great views. Once you are up on the summit, an obvious backcountry route stays at or below 4,300 feet as you ski along the east side of St. Helens through basins and across a few steep slopes and other challenges to the upper end of the Muddy River Lahar. This is all spectacular terrain with far-reaching views of Adams and Rainier. Backcountry experience and skills are required for a safe tour on this off-trail route.

Pine Marten and Sasquatch Trails to Muddy River Lahar. Although this is a 10-mile round trip, when the snow is good it is worth the effort for the views from the mile-wide mudflow. On May 18, 1980, a 30-foot wall of soil, debris, trees, and rocks mixed with melted snow and glacier ice roared down the lahar on a destructive path.

Ski the Pine Marten Trail to its end at the Sasquatch Trails, then continue on FR 83, a snowmobile route, to the lahar at 3,000 feet. Mount Adams is seen to the east, and St. Helens rises majestically from the upper end of the lahar. It is an easy, nearly level tour, but the 10-mile length requires being in good condition.

■■■■■■■■■■■■■■■■■■■■■■■■■■■■■■■■■■

40. Monitor Ridge 216H
SUMMIT CLIMB

Climb to a major volcano top, a 2,000-foot-deep crater, great views

Length ■ From Climbers' Bivouac to summit 5.8 miles
Difficulty ■ Very difficult
Users ■ Climbers properly equipped
Elevation ■ Trailhead 3,800 feet, summit 8,365 feet, elevation gain 4,565 feet
Maps ■ (Map 17), Green Trails 364S, USGS Mount St. Helens
Season ■ Late June through August
Driving Directions ■ See directions for Ptarmigan Trail (trail description 31).

An ascent to the summit of Mount St. Helens via Monitor Ridge (or any other route) is not a hike—it's a long, grueling climb over uneven, rough lava surfaces, loose rock and ash, and steep snow. St. Helens is a major peak where both weather and snow conditions often change quickly. What starts out as a nice day may change to cold, windy, and stormy weather. Be prepared to cancel your trip before you leave, or turn around on the mountain if weather threatens. Do not let the fact that more than 16,000 persons register for the climb each year mislead you into thinking this is an easy climb. Many do not make it all the way.

To ensure that your climb is safe and enjoyable, have the proper equipment. Although the climb is not steep, it may reach an angle of 35 degrees, and a small slide could get out of control. Lug-soled boots are important and clothing for cold, windy, and wet weather is always recommended. Use an ice ax, walking staff, or ski poles for balance and aid on the steeper sections and on the loose rock and pumice. In addition to icy conditions, strong, cold winds, and exposure to hypothermia, blowing dust (ash) is sometimes a problem. Ski goggles are probably the best protection for this.

Drive to the Climbers' Bivouac at the end of FR 830 (beginning of the Ptarmigan Trail). It has parking and restrooms. Dispersed camping at the parking lot is permitted. Water is not available, so be sure to carry lots of water as the ash and grit-covered snow on the route is not suitable as a water source.

The Climbers' Bivouac may be blocked early in the season by snow

Panorama from crater rim of Mount St. Helens showing crater, lava dome, Pumice Plain, Spirit Lake, Johnston Ridge, Mount Rainier, Goat Rocks range, and Mount Adams (David Duck)

banks. Hike up the Ptarmigan Trail 2.1 miles, cross the Loowit Trail, then continue 300 yards into the basin at the edge of forest and at the foot of a high lava flow. Tall posts mark the trail as it climbs steeply up the face of the flow to its top. You have two alternatives: climb the lava ridge, often snow free, or drop west off the ridge onto snow and parallel it upward, a route considered by many to be easier in early season. In May and early June, the mountain is a snow climb, so bring good boots, rope, crampons, and ice ax. A rope may not be necessary technically, but in the event of whiteout or fog it will be a valuable way to keep a party together.

If you choose the ridge, follow the marked trail up the lava flow along the side of Point 5,994, the prominent high point on the ridge to your right. Struggle up the loose rock and sand and gain a series of rocky steps or bulges, each about 100 feet high, that require scrambling up and over boulders.

Once up this section, gain a wide, rounded, gentle ridge of loose, sandy, volcanic ash and pumice, which in early summer is often snow covered. Follow this to the summit rim where most climbers congregate. The true high point is about 1,200 feet farther west and is reached

by traversing across and down at the head of the Dryer Glacier and climbing steep snow and loose rocky slopes.

Be cautious at the crater's edge as there is often an overhanging snow cornice that may be cantilevered up to 40 feet out from the rim, creating a highly dangerous situation for anyone venturing onto it. Do not walk on snow to the crater's edge unless you know it is safe. If there is no snow cornice, be aware that the snow-free edge of the crater rim is itself unstable and dangerous. In late summer there is often a dangerous snow shelf below the rim. Do not climb down and onto this for better views. Walk west along the rim for better views and to appreciate the curve of the rim with Adams rising above it.

When descending the mountain some climbers will avoid the pumice and ash and descend snow-filled gullies to the west of the ridge. If you do, always keep close or within sight of the ridge or you may miss the Ptarmigan Trail. However, if you follow the fall line down it will lead you unconsciously westward and away from the safe route, which may result in a long, nasty descent through brush and thick forest until you reach a lower road, perhaps hours later than if you had carefully descended on route.

Southwest Climbing Route. The most convenient access to the routes on this side of the mountain is via Butte Camp Trail 238A from Redrock Pass with a camp at Lower Butte Camp meadow (4,000 feet). There are no suitable campsites above here, and camping and off-trail travel are discouraged in the Loowit Trail area. Climbing here should be done on this side only when the ground is covered by snow to avoid damage to research areas and to sensitive natural features. Above the Loowit the climbing route goes straight up on slopes that are about the same angle of steepness as those of the Monitor Ridge route.

Mount St. Helens North

Goat Creek Trail

■ ■

For hikers seeking less-used trails that offer isolation, the north end provides that opportunity. The 30-odd miles of this region's trails include approach hikes through lovely forest. The three principal trail systems here are Vanson Peak–Deadmans Lake–Goat Mountain Ridge, Goat Creek–Cathedral Falls–Tumwater Mountain, and the trails of the Ryan Lake area. The first two trail systems are reached from logging company roads. These three trail systems are connected, and there are opportunities for easy hikes and long, demanding one-day hikes, as well as backpacking into the long loops and scenic, high-ridge trails.

■ ACCESS ■

Access to this area southwest of Randle was seriously affected by the February 1996 flood damage to FR 26, which has been closed ever since and which may be reopened in 1997 or 1998. It therefore became a high priority to open FR 25, which accesses the popular Windy Ridge viewpoints and trails. If reopened, FR 26 will give access to the south end of these trail systems from the Ryan Lake area.

From Seattle/Tacoma. Drive I-5 south and in Tacoma take Exit 133. Drive Highway 7 to Morton, 90 miles from Seattle. From Morton drive east 5.0 miles and turn south onto Kosmos Road, go 0.1 mile, turn left onto 100 Champion Haul Road, and drive 4.2 miles on the gravel to a bridge over Riffe Lake. For further directions, and from the town of Randle, see driving directions for Goat Creek Trail (trail description 41).

From Portland/Vancouver. Drive I-5 68 miles north from the Columbia River bridge to Exit 68 and onto Highway 12, then 31 miles east to Morton. From Morton follow same directions as above.

■ RECREATION OPPORTUNITIES ■

The north side of the monument offers no skiing or climbing. Recreation opportunities are limited to hiking and mountain biking. There are beautiful old-growth forests here for the nature lover.

■■■■■■■■■■■■■■■■■■■■■■■■■■■■■■■■■

41. Goat Creek Trail 205 to Cathedral Falls

Perhaps the most interesting and beautiful green forest trail in the monument

Length ■ Lower section 2.9 miles
Difficulty ■ Moderate
Users ■ Hikers, Mountain bikers
Elevation ■ Trailhead 2,400 feet, Goat Creek crossing 2,800 feet at hike end
Maps ■ (Map 21), Green Trails 332, USGS Vanson Peak, Cowlitz Falls
Season ■ Late June through October
Driving Directions ■ From Randle drive west on Highway 12 for 12 miles and turn south onto Kosmos Road; go 0.1 mile, turn left onto 100 Champion Haul Road, and drive 4.2 miles on gravel to a bridge over Riffe Lake. Just prior to the bridge pass the entrance to Taidnapam Park, a quality public utilities campground. From Morton on Highway 12 drive east 5 miles to Kosmos Road and follow previous directions; turn right on the far side of the bridge, and drive 0.8 mile to FR 2750 (may not be marked), turn left and follow this road 4 miles on a wide, one-lane, smooth gravel surface to the trailhead. (This road was damaged by 1996 landslides. Call Randle Ranger District to verify it is driveable. If not, it can be biked to the trailhead.)

From the trailhead climb gentle grades along the west side of Goat Creek far above the valley bottom, and soon enter beautiful old-growth forest on the steep mountainside. At 0.4 mile pass a shallow cave. Along this steep hillside the trail is ledgelike, winding along and climbing moderately as it passes through a pristine, quiet virgin forest of towering trees.

Pass a side stream and continue on the wrinkled hillside with ups and downs, then make a significant climb past an unusual, vertical, moss-covered rock slab. A steep 400-yard climb leads into a small side basin just over a mile from the trailhead. Here a massive, rounded cliff hangs over the trail and a wispy waterfall cascades from the forest fringe far above. The enormous overhang creates an alcove of giant proportions where mosses, greenery, and tall cedars flourish under the sheltering bulge. The alcove, in reality a giant grotto, is almost 100 feet deep, and the trail passes behind the waterfall. Cool breezes are created by the cascading water. This is an exquisite site, and a unique feature of the monument.

Continue, and soon the trail regains its ledgelike route then passes several stream crossings with lovely cascades. You will see a waterfall below on Goat Creek. Deer ferns are trailside with their slender black stems rising from the center of their fronds.

At 2 miles reach a junction, where Goat Creek Trail goes steeply uphill 4 miles to join the Goat Mountain Trail. Continue on the lower trail, now Tumwater Trail 218, cross two creeks near the junction, and climb through old growth. See a nursery log suspended far above and

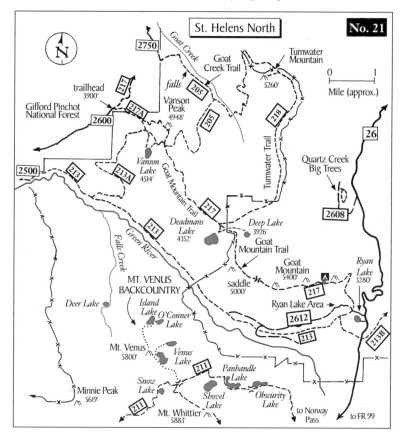

crossing Goat Creek. Large amounts of pumice from ancient eruptions are falling onto the trail from trailside cutbanks in addition to what you see along the trail from the 1980 eruption.

Climbing steadily reach the creek crossing at 2,800 feet on slabby, gray rocks where in early season a crossing might be a problem with high water. Across the creek, Trail 218 climbs relentlessly to the summit of Tumwater Mountain and then south and west along a scenic ridgeline. The Goat Creek crossing is an ideal place to have lunch before you turn around to head back. Enjoy the rock slabs that provide perfect places to sit as you enjoy the beauty of the place. Just below the crossing is a long, deep, clear pool for swimming. If you are adventuresome, go 80 yards upstream to a lovely pool fed by cascades.

Mountain Biking. The trail tread is compact and mostly free from obstacles, but there are steep trailside dropoffs in places. The trail to the lunch stop has a few steep climbs, but the upper Goat Creek and Tumwater Trails are very steep and demanding.

42. Vanson Peak–
Goat Mountain Trails 217-3,
217A, 217-2, 217-1

Forest hiking to a former lookout site, lakes, and a high, scenic ridge

Length ▪ Vanson Peak Summit 2.3 miles, Goat Mountain Saddle 6.5 miles one way
Difficulty ▪ Difficult
Users ▪ Hikers, Mountain bikers, Backpackers
Elevation ▪ Trailhead 3,900 feet, Vanson Peak Summit 4,498 feet, Goat Mountain Saddle 5,000 feet
Cumulative Gain ▪ Round trip to Goat Mountain Saddle 3,000 feet
Maps ▪ (Map 21), Green Trails 332, USGS Vanson Peak, Cowlitz Falls
Season ▪ Late June through October
Driving Directions ▪ See Goat Creek Trail directions (trail description 41). Cross the bridge over Riffe Lake, turn right and follow a

confusing complex of gravel roads with several junctions; the Vanson Peak trailhead is 13 miles from the bridge, an easy, gradual climb of 3,100 feet. Although you will pass numerous side roads on the drive to Vanson Peak there are only two critical junctions, both Y-shaped, and at each you go left, uphill. These two are 7.1 miles (signs) and 10.3 miles (unmarked) from the Riffe Lake bridge; follow always what is the main, widest, most used route. At about 1 mile beyond the second Y the road narrows briefly, becomes steeper, and is quite rough for 100 yards or so. (You may want to ask passengers to walk if you are driving a low-clearance vehicle; otherwise the road is quite good). About 0.5 mile above the rough section pass an inverted Y-shaped junction, then a second one nearby with a watertank. You are now only 0.8 mile from an unlogged point of forest; another 200 yards bring you to the trailhead, where there is a horse loading ramp and hitching rail. (None of the gravel roads you have driven are Forest Service roads; they belong to Champion International, which has no obligation to mark roads for recreational users.) *An alternative driving route for hikers from Portland/Vancouver and Longview*, and shorter than driving Highway 12, follows I-5, then Highway 504 toward the Coldwater Ridge Visitor Center. At milepost 25 leave 504 and drive Weyerhaeuser Road 2500 (sign), then Road 2600 to the trailhead, a total of about 28 miles. (Washouts in 1996 closed the road, and the future for use of this road by recreational users is not clear. Call the Weyerhaeuser Company in Longview, Washington, to determine if the road is open to recreational use or closed due to washouts or fire danger.)

From the trailhead the most rewarding hiking route is up Vanson Peak for its sweeping views and then on to your other goals. If you are carrying an overnight pack, hike to the four-way junction, drop your pack, and take the short trail directly to the summit.

Goat Mountain Saddle, a must for most hikers, is 6.5 miles from the trailhead. Continuing even a bit farther is worthwhile. On the way, make a side trip for lunch to Deadmans Lake. If you cannot make it to the saddle on Goat Mountain, at least go 1.3 miles beyond the lake for the stunning views from the high, open hillside under towering cliffs.

To start your trip, hike up from the trailhead through the clearcut with views of Rainier and to Riffe Lake to the west and 3,200 feet below. In 500 yards enter the forest, then take the side trail (217A) to the summit as it climbs seriously to the ridge crest, then left 300 yards to the top. Riffe Lake and Rainier are seen as well as Tumwater

Goat Mountain Saddle with scorched trees. From Deadmans Lake the trail climbs to the saddle up the hillside on the right.

Mountain to the east above the deep Goat Creek valley. Then Adams appears, while St. Helens is partially hidden behind Mount Venus. The foreground ridge between Adams and St. Helens comes off Tumwater Mountain with its ridge-top trail to Deadmans Lake. Above and beyond are two prominent high points, both part of Goat Mountain, and between them is the saddle you should attempt to reach. Near the lookout site find Indian paintbrush, phlox, delicate, small harebell, clover, lupine, and daisies.

   Take the south ridge trail down to a four-way junction with the Goat Creek Trail. Go straight along the ridge crest, climb into meadows with no views, descend steeply, then climb and descend another ridge high point into a broad, forested saddle where the Tumwater Mountain Trail joins. Nearby Deadmans Lake has good tent sites, a toilet, and a sandy beach. This is the best basecamp location for a one-day hike to Tumwater Mountain and back, and to Goat Mountain Saddle. The Tumwater hike has a cumulative elevation gain of 2,000 feet or so with the trail's many ups and downs.

Deadmans Lake on the Goat Mountain Trail

Continue to Goat Mountain and enjoy the splendid views as you get higher onto open slopes before reaching the saddle, a rewarding goal by itself. At the saddle stand scorched, bleached trees from the eruption blast, and below to the north are areas of scorched trees almost surrounded by surviving green forest. The view across the glacial, U-shaped Green River valley is of the Mount Margaret Backcountry and its many peaks. You will not see the several lakes, but the cirque cliffs above are visible. Whittier Mountain, the central long ridge, hides Mount Margaret. Pleasant Pass is the deep notch to the right, and farther right is the forested and partially scorched Mount Venus. Blowdown forest litters the backcountry slopes. In another direction, far to the left is the long ridge of Strawberry Mountain.

If you have time, hike the trail eastward across grassy hillsides into the green forest near the east end of the Goat Mountain ridge. It is a marvelous, scenic, nearly level hike.

On your return to the trailhead, drop into Vanson Lake. The first trail (217C) into the lake from the trailhead leads to an uninteresting, inaccessible lakeshore and mediocre campsites. A second trail, unsigned, steeper, and farther south on the main trail, leads to the best campsites.

Mountain Biking. The entire distance from the trailhead has a firm, good tread but is steep in many places. There are few rocks, roots, and water bars. From Goat Mountain Saddle and east, in many places the trail is frothy with soft deposits of pumice.

■■

43. Quartz Creek Big Trees 219

A short, barrier-free loop through giant trees and lovely trailside greenery

👫 ♿

Length ■ Loop 0.5 mile
Difficulty ■ Easy, for wheelchair users some steep sections
Users ■ Hikers, Wheelchair users
Elevation ■ Trail 1,960 feet
Maps ■ (Map 21), Green Trails 332
Season ■ April through October
Driving Directions ■ From Randle drive FR 25 south 10 miles to FR 26, follow FR 26 for 8 miles to FR 2608, a gravel side road that goes 1 mile to the Big Trees loop (FR 26, a wide, one-lane road with turnouts, was badly damaged in February 1996 by many washouts and landslides and it may be 1998 before it is reopened. It can be biked, but until reopened it is too far to hike. Some washouts removed the entire road surface and may be difficult to get around if further damage occurs. The bridge on FR 2608 at Quartz Creek, 0.4 mile from FR 26, was washed out and may never be repaired or reopened. Check with the Randle Ranger District office to verify road conditions.)

At the trailhead to the old-growth loop, follow the compacted gravel path clockwise and enter the realm of great trees, some up to 10 feet in diameter and 250 feet tall. As you walk the trail go between two 8-foot giants, cross a boggy area on a boardwalk, and pass a 9-foot ancient specimen with a smaller tree attached and holding on with an octopuslike grip. At a bench enclosed by three giants, sit and quietly enjoy the magnificent trees, some 650 years old.

The mixture of smaller trees with large ones accents the enormous size of the giants. Look for the trailside big cedar with a smaller tree literally growing from within its folds.

Goat Mountain seen from Strawberry Mountain. Ryan Lake area is right of center in road curve, and Goat Mountain Trail climbs through forest to ridgetop.

44. Ryan Lake Area

A deep U-shaped river valley, old growth, high-ridge walks, sweeping views

Length ▪ Green River Trail 213 9.6 miles, Vanson Ridge Trail 213A 3.3 miles, Goat Mountain Trail 217 to views 3 miles, Greenberry Trail 217 3.8 miles

Difficulty ▪ Moderate for all trails up to 7 miles one way, Difficult beyond 7 miles

Users ▪ Hikers

Elevation ▪ Ryan Lake 3,280 feet, trail junction with 213A 2,300 feet

Maps ▪ (Maps 9, 21), Green Trails 332, USGS Spirit Lake East, Vanson Peak, Cowlitz Falls

Season ▪ Late June through September

Driving Directions ▪ Drive FR 26 from Randle 21 miles to Ryan Lake, or drive FR 26 from FR 99 past Norway Pass trailhead 5

miles to Ryan Lake, then drive FR 2612 about 0.5 mile to the Horse Camp, which is the trailhead for the Green River, Goat Mountain, and Greenberry Trails. (Due to extensive damage to FR 26 by the February 1996 storms, this road is closed and may never be repaired or reopened. Call the Packwood Ranger District for road information.)

Green River Trail. From the Horse Camp hike down the wide, impressive U-shaped valley of the Green River, formed 12,000 years ago by an immense glacier. Ryan Lake and the first part of the trail are in the blow-down zone and trees here were salvage logged. The trail parallels FR 2612 for 2.8 miles along the north side of the river. FR 2612 is driveable to where it turns. If you have driven, this is where you find the trail for hiking. Ryan Lake and FR 2612 are not in the monument; however, the trail eventually crosses into the monument and old-growth forest about 1.8 mile beyond the turn in FR 2612. On the trail you pass historic sites of former mines: Polar Star and Minnie Lee. At 7 miles reach Vanson Ridge Trail 213A. In the last 2 miles, past the Minnie Lee mine site, there are good campsites and small beaches along the river. Beyond the Vanson Ridge Trail, the Green River Trail continues 2.5 miles to Weyerhaeuser Road 2500 and the monument's west boundary.

Devils club and ferns on Quartz Creek Big Trees loop

Vanson Ridge Trail. This 3.3-mile trail climbs to its upper end through deep forest at the Goat Mountain Trail west of Vanson Lake. The moderately steep trail takes you to a viewpoint and a waterfall along the way. If you are a strong hiker, you may want to make an 18.5-mile loop by returning to the Horse Camp on the Goat Mountain Trail. Cumulative elevation gain is about 3,400 feet.

Goat Mountain Trail. From the Horse Camp climb the south side of Goat Mountain on steep grades, at first through a blow-down area, then into green forest. At 4,200 feet the trail turns westward, and you cross a high point at 5,100 feet, for a gain of 1,720 feet. Descend open slopes onto a beautiful sidehill route through mixed green meadows and stands of alpine fir. Leave the trees to cross vast, flowered slopes with views across the entire sweep of the Mount Margaret Backcountry peaks. At 3 miles reach Goat Mountain Saddle with wonderful views east, south, and north. (See trail description 42 for more information.)

Greenberry Trail. This trail climbs 3.8 miles to the 4,800-foot ridge top north of the former fire lookout site on Strawberry Mountain. The highest point along the long ridge is 5,739 feet and 2 miles north of the viewpoint lookout site. Hike south along a rolling trail with many views, passing through the scorched zone, then dead forest and open areas with many views. Continue to the 4,854-foot saddle on FR 2516, the parking place for hikers to Strawberry Mountain. From here it is only 0.7 mile to the summit, accumulated elevation gain from Ryan Lake about 2,400 feet. (See trail description 7 for more information.)

One of many washouts on Forest Road 26 from February 1996 storms

Acknowledgments

■ ■

Jim Nieland, Recreation Planner and Walt Doan, Forest Service volunteer, both of Monument headquarters, and Jim Quiring, Director, Coldwater Ridge Visitor Center, were particularly helpful in providing information and reviewing much of this guide. In addition, at headquarters, Hans Castren, Mika Asikainen, Juli Bradley, all backcountry rangers, and Teresa Newton were very helpful.

Other Forest Service personnel who provided information were: James Slagle, Gifford Pinchot National Forest headquarters; Dave Olson, Randle Ranger District; Bonnie Lippitt, Visitor Centers Director, Mount St. Helens Visitor Center; Debi Church, Coldwater Ridge Visitor Center.

David Wieprecht, Cascades Volcano Observatory, and Austin Post, U.S. Geological Survey, were helpful, and advice was appreciated from Keith Mischke, Vera Dafoe, and John Haek. Computer assistance and support from my wife, Nancy Chapman, was most helpful.

Resources

■ ■

The author would like to acknowledge his heavy reliance on Patrick T. Pringle's excellent book, *Roadside Geology of Mount St. Helens National Volcanic Monument and Vicinity* (Olympia, Wash: Department of Natural Resources, 1993) while doing research for this book. This small volume, at $5.95, is an essential for all visitors to the monument. For information, list of publications, or use of the Department of Natural Resources library, call (360) 902-1450.

■ ADDRESSES ■

Mount St. Helens National Volcanic Monument
42218 Northeast Yale Bridge Road
Amboy, WA 98601

(360) 247-3900 (Information 7:30–5:00 P.M. weekdays)
(360) 247-3903 (24-hour recording)
(360) 247-3961 (climbing hotline)

Mount St. Helens Visitor Center (Silver Lake)
Johnston Ridge Observatory
3029 Spirit Lake Highway
Castle Rock, WA 98611
(360) 274-2100 (information)
(360) 274-2103 (24-hour recording)

Coldwater Ridge Visitor Center
3029 Spirit Lake Highway
Castle Rock, WA 98611
(360) 274-2131 (information)

Gifford Pinchot National Forest
Forest Headquarters
10600 NE 51st Street
P.O. Box 8944
Vancouver, WA 98682
(360) 891-5000 (information)
(360) 891-5009 (24-hour recording)

Randle Ranger District
P.O. Box 670
Randle, WA 98377
(360) 497-1100 (information)

Snow Avalanche and Weather Information
(503) 326-2400 (24-hour recorded information)

Washington State Campground Reservations
(800) 452-5687 (reservations)
(800) 233-0321 (information)

Weyerhaeuser Company
 (360) 414-3441
(360) 425-2150 (recording)

Index

■ ■

About the Author

Author and outdoor enthusiast Klindt Vielbig has been an avid hiker, climber, and skier for nearly fifty years. His passion for the outdoors has taken him to the backcountry on countless adventures: he has climbed actively in the Cascade Mountains for more than twenty-five years; he has undertaken numerous backpacking and hiking excursions in southern Washington and Oregon; and he has cross-country skied since 1965, organizing the first Nordic ski school on the West Coast.

Vielbig is a long-time member of the Mazamas, the Trails Club of Oregon, the Sierra Club, the Audubon Society, and the Nature Conservancy, as well as a charter member of the Oregon Nordic Club. An Oregon native, Vielbig is the author of the popular *Cross-Country Ski Routes: Oregon and Southwest Washington*. He lives in Portland, Oregon.

Other titles you may enjoy from The Mountaineers:

CROSS-COUNTRY SKI ROUTES: Oregon, *Klindt Vielbig*
Includes 500 trails covering over 2,000 miles! Descriptions and maps for beginning to advanced tours, with new information on backcountry trips for experienced wilderness skiers. Includes tours in SW Washington.

HIKING OREGON'S GEOLOGY, *Ellen Morris Bishop & John Eliot Allen*
Guide to Oregon's most scenic and geologically interesting places offers information to help you understand the state's geologic history. Hikes range from strolls in urban parks to wilderness summit climbs.

A GUIDE TO WASHINGTON'S SOUTH CASCADES' VOLCANIC LANDSCAPES, *Marge & Ted Mueller*
Compilation of adventures for explorers interested in the volcanic history of more than 80 South Cascadian volcanic sites, including Mount Adams, Mount Rainier, and Mount St. Helens.

EXPLORING WASHINGTON'S WILD AREAS: A Guide for Hikers, Backpackers, Climbers, X-C Skiers, & Paddlers, *Marge & Ted Mueller*
Guide to 55 wilderness areas with outstanding recreational opportunities, plus notes on history, geology, plants and animals, and wildlife.

WASHINGTON STATE PARKS: A Complete Recreation Guide, *Marge & Ted Mueller*
Comprehensive guide to hiking, camping, boating, and picnicking opportunities in Washington's breathtaking state parks.

COLUMBIA RIVER GORGE: A Complete Guide, *Philip N. Jones, Editor*
Information on hiking, cycling, windsurfing, boating, camping, and photography opportunities. Covers history, weather, geology, and flora and fauna.

50 HIKES IN MOUNT RAINIER NATIONAL PARK, 3rd Ed., *Ira Spring & Harvey Manning*

100 HIKES IN WASHINGTON'S ALPINE LAKES, 2nd Ed., *Ira Spring, Harvey Manning, & Vicky Spring*

100 HIKES IN WASHINGTON'S GLACIER PEAK REGION: THE NORTH CASCADES, 3rd Ed., *Ira Spring & Harvey Manning*

100 HIKES IN WASHINGTON'S NORTH CASCADES NATIONAL PARK REGION, 2nd Ed., *Ira Spring & Harvey Manning*

100 HIKES IN WASHINGTON'S SOUTH CASADES AND OLYMPICS, 2nd Ed., *Ira Spring & Harvey Manning*

THE MOUNTAINEERS, founded in 1906, is a nonprofit outdoor activity and conservation club, whose mission is "to explore, study, preserve, and enjoy the natural beauty of the outdoors. . . ." Based in Seattle, Washington, the club is now the third-largest such organization in the United States, with 15,000 members and five branches throughout Washington State.

The Mountaineers sponsors both classes and year-round outdoor activities in the Pacific Northwest, which include hiking, mountain climbing, ski-touring, snowshoeing, bicycling, camping, kayaking and canoeing, nature study, sailing, and adventure travel. The club's conservation division supports environmental causes through educational activities, sponsoring legislation, and presenting informational programs. All club activities are led by skilled, experienced volunteers, who are dedicated to promoting safe and responsible enjoyment and preservation of the outdoors.

If you would like to participate in these organized outdoor activities or the club's programs, consider a membership in The Mountaineers. For information and an application, write or call The Mountaineers, Club Headquarters, 300 Third Avenue West, Seattle, Washington 98119; (206) 284-6310.

The Mountaineers Books, an active, nonprofit publishing program of the club, produces guidebooks, instructional texts, historical works, natural history guides, and works on environmental conservation. All books produced by The Mountaineers are aimed at fulfilling the club's mission.

Send or call for our catalog of more than 300 outdoor titles:

 The Mountaineers Books
1001 SW Klickitat Way, Suite 201
Seattle, WA 98134
1-800-553-4453 / e-mail: mbooks@mountaineers.org